Shakespeare

GAMES

All the world's a stage. And all the men and women merely players.
The idea of the Seven Ages of Man, expressed so eloquently by Jaques in
As You Like It, was not original with Shakespeare.
The above illustration of the same theme is from
a mid-fifteenth-century woodcut in the British Museum
reproduced in *Archaeologia*, Vol. 35 (1853,
Folger Library copy.)

Shakespeare
GAMES

ROBERT FENSTER

HARMONY BOOKS
NEW YORK

Book designed by Constance T. Doyle

Published by Harmony Books,
a division of Crown Publishers, Inc.,
One Park Avenue, New York, New York 10016
and simultaneously in Canada by General Publishing Company, Ltd.

HARMONY BOOKS and colophon are trademarks of Crown Publishers, Inc.

Manufactured in the United States of America

Library of Congress Cataloging in Publication Data
Fenster, Robert.
Shakespeare games.
1. Shakespeare, William, 1564–1616—Miscellanea.
2. Literary recreations.   3. Word games.   I. Title.
PR2773.F46   1982   822.3'3   81-20105
                                      AACR2

ISBN: 0-517-54623X cloth
       0-517-546248 paper

10 9 8 7 6 5 4 3 2 1
First Edition

for
MARGOT AND DAVE BOTSFORD,
who have wonderful taste in gifts

CONTENTS

A N S W E R S

INTRODUCTION

"This way, my lord," the Huntsman in *King Henry the Sixth* says, "for this way lies the game."

There is nothing in life better than a good game—except a better game. If life had any sense at all, the world would be board-shaped and we would be born with silver dice in our hands. The play, after all, is the thing.

In preparation for this book of games, I read Shakespeare forward and backward until I arrived, one midsummer's night, at that dreamlike crystallization of Shakespearean investigation: a Shakespearean theory to call my own.

My theory is that the Bard himself made up the games you are about to play in this book. Bemused magician that he was, Shakespeare then hid the puzzles inside his plays and poems, knowing that one day someone would come along and recover them. So the gauntlet is thrown down to all of you Shakespearean detectives to disprove my theory if you can. Games are for the playing, so turn the page and "play out the play." For, as Belarius in *Cymbeline* says, "The game is up!"

Gamesters take note: The games are loosely arranged in order of ascending difficulty. Although there are tough ones strewn throughout the book, the last section is the most difficult.

Bonus Game: Some of the game titles are actual Shakespearean quotations; some are paraphrases. Pick out the real quotations from the paraphrases.

Bonus points if you can identify the quotations from which the paraphrases are drawn.

Coronets awarded to military victors.
From Claude Guichard, *Funerailles & diverses manieres* (1581).

SCORING

Score five points for each correct answer. There are 517 correct answers in the book; a perfect score is 2,585. Bonus points are scored as indicated for individual games.

How do you rate your Shakespearean scholarship?

Points	Rating	Quote
2,585+	Excellent	O, wonderful, wonderful, and most wonderful, wonderful! and yet again wonderful, and after that, out of all whooping! (Celia, *As You Like It*, Act 3, Scene 2)
1,750	Very good	One that excels the quirks of blazoning pens. (Cassio, *Othello*, Act 2, Scene 1)
1,250	Good	A hit, a very palpable hit. (Osric, *Hamlet*, Act 5, Scene 2)
1,000	Fair	The hand that hath made you fair hath made you good. (Vincentio, *Measure for Measure*, Act 3, Scene 1)
750	Average	So-so is good, very good, very excellent good: and yet it is not; it is but so-so. (Touchstone, *As You Like It*, Act 5, Scene 1)
0	Nothing	Nothing will come of nothing. (Lear, *King Lear*, Act 1, Scene 1)

Hector and Ajax.
From Lodovico Dolce, *Le transformationi* (1570).

GAMES

G A M E

1

The play's the thing

EACH SPEECH in the following scene is an opening line from one of Shakespeare's plays. Name each speaker and the play.

1. "Who's there?"

2. "Boatswain!"

3. "Good day, sir."

4. "Good morrow, and well met. How have ye done, since last we saw in France?"

5. "You do not meet a man but frowns: our bloods no more obey the heavens, than our courtiers still seem as does the king's."

6. "I thought the king had more affected the Duke of Albany than Cornwall."

7. "Nay, but this dotage of our general's o'erflows the measure."

8. "I wonder how the king escaped our hands."

9. "Escalus—"

10. "Open your ears; for which of you will stop the vent of hearing when loud Rumour speaks?"

11. "Cease to persuade, my loving Proteus: Home-keeping youth have ever homely wits."

12. "Noble patricians, patrons of my right, defend the justice of my cause with arms."

13. "Sir Hugh, persuade me not; I will make a Star-Chamber matter of it."

14. "Before we proceed any further, hear me speak."

15. "If music be the food of love, play on."

16. "I learn in this letter that Don Pedro of Arragon comes this night to Messina."

17. "Proceed, Solinus, to procure my fall, and by the doom of death end woes and all."

18. "Let fame, that all hunt after in their lives, live registered upon our brazen tombs."

19. "Hence! home, you idle creatures, get you home: Is this a holiday?"

20. "When shall we three meet again in thunder, lightning, or in rain?"

21. "In Troy, there lies the scene."

G A M E

2

Methodical madness

UNSCRAMBLE the anagrams to form the titles of some of Shakespeare's plays.

Example: THE LAM—Hamlet

1. LET'S WIN THEATRE
2. NAME DUET ROIL JO
3. SEW HER HOT FAT GEM THIN
4. GRAIN ELK
5. SAUCER JAIL US
6. REUSE FAME USE ARMOR
7. HERO FORMS CODE TREY
8. HOLE LOT
9. YES AUK I TOIL
10. HOT GUM BOAT UNDO CHAIN
11. OF THIN MAN TOES
12. HEP TEST MET

G A M E
3
Disordered wit

THESE SCRAMBLED lines contain all the words of familiar Shakespearean lines. Put the words in the correct order, then name the speaker and the play.

Example: In rotten choice, there's small apples.—"There's small choice in rotten apples." (Hortensio, *The Taming of the Shrew*)

1. Though thou art thyself, thy name is not a Montague; but that 'tis my enemy.

2. Not from heaven is the mercy beneath; rain droppeth as the gentle quality, strained of the place upon it.

3. Glorious summer, by York, made of this winter; now our discontent is of the sun.

4. What men abide needs that must impose fates.

5. Therefore, to be a woman she is beautiful, and therefore she's won to be woo'd.

6. Two rough, ready pilgrims that stand blushing; to smooth my lips, kiss with a tender touch.
   Pilgrim, do good; you hand your wrong too much.

7. Proud England, the conqueror of a foot, did lie at this, nor never shall never.

8. He found his way, and it lay in rebellion.

9. Brutus stars; is not the fault in our dear.

10. When they are men they woo; when April wed December.

11. Men forget the best, but are sometimes men.

12. Sins love the few; to act, to hear, they love.

Yorick, the King's jester.
From Olaus Magnus, *Historia de gentibus septentrionalibus* (1555).

G A M E
4
A sea of choices

EVERY WORDSMITH is faced with a sea of choices. If you're a Shakespeare, you make the right ones. If you're not, you come up with lines like the ones below. Rewrite these lines into familiar Shakespearean prose.

Bonus Points: 5 points for identifying both the speaker and the play.

Example: Frangibility, your cognomen is distaff.— "Frailty, thy name is woman." (Hamlet, *Hamlet*)

1. Rivet your mettle to the agglutinating location.

2. Disjointure is such dulcet contrition that I shall utter adieu till it be *mañana.*

3. He cerebrates excessively: Such blokes are perilous.

4. Somnolence that vamps the draggletailed webwork of botheration.

5. My slaw period wherein I was raw in illation.

6. But I will accouter my idolatry upon my armlet for simpletons to nibble at.

7. An individual that doted upon not sagaciously but inordinately competent.

8. But do I eye askance your essence, it is exceedingly packed with the serous fluid of hominoidal altruism.

9. How more acuminated than an ophidian's denticle it is to have an ungrateful scion.

10. Gagged with aspiration of the more ignoble variety.

11. Reiterate, lucid seraph!

12. Poltroons perish copious iterations preceding their cessation; the doughty on no occasion enter into the spirit of extinction but for the nonce.

An alchemist experimenting.
From Konrad Gesner, *The New Jewel of Health* (1576).

G R A P H I C   G A M E
1
To be or not to be

STARTING from the arrow, find Hamlet by following his famous speech through the maze, on pages 9–11.

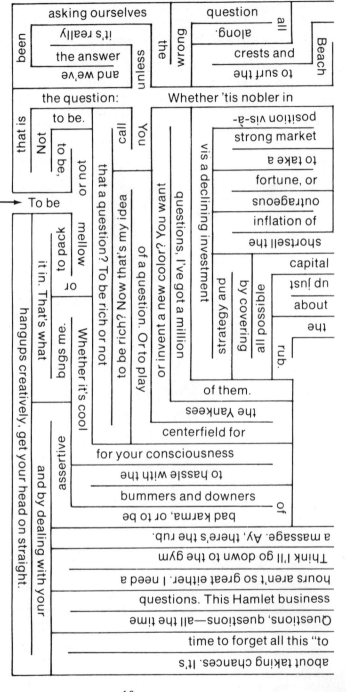

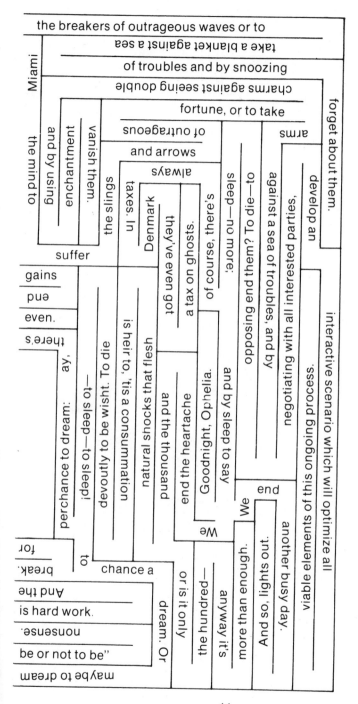

G A M E
5
Confuse thy name

UNSCRAMBLE the anagrams to form the names of some of Shakespeare's characters.
Example: LONE OAT—Leonato

1. AIL HOPE
2. RIP TOUCHE
3. FAT LAFFS
4. NO MAD SEED
5. LEND TRUE SIGN
6. I SOLO PUN
7. O NIX SLEEP
8. ANTILOVE
9. NO CUTE SHOT
10. BY HATED CLAM
11. REAL TRUE FOG CLOSE
12. RAGED
13. AIR TOP
14. DEAR TIP
15. LIVEN ANTE
16. LEAD FOR OWN LUCK
17. POT RUSH
18. LIVE BOON
19. MOB TOT
20. CLAUSES
21. SUPER TO
22. PA NO HINT
23. I BORN
24. CARD SOT
25. RAIL NOSE
26. A RASH BLAT
27. LIVER GNATS
28. INTO SHORE
29. ODD PRONE
30. ERR BY GOD
31. SPRITES GAMES
32. SATIN BASE
33. GIN LORE
34. TALC OPERA
35. MA ROAD

G A M E

6

Deceitful words

CHOOSE CORRECT meanings for these words; each is taken from a Shakespearean quotation.

Bonus Points: 5 points for naming the speaker of each line; 5 points for identifying the play.

1. *jets:* "Contemplation makes a rare turkey-cock of him: How he jets under his advanced plumes!"
    a. sheds thoughts   c. struts
    b. flies in one's dreams d. sweats

2. *kerns:* "We must supplant these rough rug-headed kerns, which live like venom, where no venom else but only they have privilege to live."
    a. poisonous plants
    b. nobles opposed to the king
    c. London squatters known for sleeping on the floor
    d. lightly armed footsoldiers

3. *horologe:* " 'Tis evermore the prologue to his sleep: He'll watch the horologe a double set, if drink rock not his cradle."
    a. a bad play
    b. a clock
    c. an early version of tennis
    d. a slide show of someone's vacation

4. *mop:* "Each one, tripping one his toe, will be here with mop and mow."
    a. a festival hat
    b. a grimace

c. a cow with a long tail that drags on the ground

d. a dry broom used before floors were cleaned with water

5. *yerkt:* "Nine or ten times I had thought t'have yerkt him here under the ribs."

a. shoved

b. tickled

c. jerked

d. carved

6. *ostent:* "Use all the observance of civility, like one well studied in a sad ostent."

a. a clerical job

b. a school so poor it couldn't afford buildings but gave classes in tents

c. a display

d. a school of acting that taught only the tragedies

7. *neif:* "Sweet knight, I kiss thy neif: What! We have seen the seven stars."

a. fist

b. knee

c. female astrologer

d. niece

8. *weet:* "And such a twain can do't, in which I bind, on pain of punishment, the world to weet we stand up peerless."

a. weep

b. provide with grain

c. acknowledge kingship

d. know

9. *bed-presser:* "This sanguine coward, this bed-presser, this horse-back-breaker, this huge hill of flesh."

a. innkeeper

b. lazy fellow

c. paramour

d. angel of death

10. *fap:* "And being fap, sir, was, as they say, cashiered; and so conclusions passed the careires."

    a. out of shape   c. drunk

    b. wealthy   d. daring

11. *infamonize:* "Dost thou infamonize me among potentates?"

    a. defame

    b. praise

    c. put on a strict diet

    d. imitate rudely

12. *elder-gun:* "That's a perilous shot out of an elder-gun, that a poor and a private displeasure can do against a monarch!"

    a. an old man's weapon

    b. a harmless weapon

    c. a sharp tongue

    d. a cannon

13. *palter:* "And be these juggling fiends no more believed, that palter with us in a double sense."

    a. make puns   c. dance

    b. juggle   d. use trickery

14. *tuition:* "I have almost matter enough in me for such an embassage; and so I commit you—" "To the tuition of God."

    a. penitence

    b. a lunatic asylum

    c. protection

    d. God's finishing school, i.e., the Earth

15. *gamester:* "She's impudent, my lord, and was a common gamester to the camp."

    a. puzzle maker

    b. someone who accepts dares

    c. lewd person

    d. poacher

G A M E

7

Star-crossed lovers

REUNITE these lost lovers:
>Romeo and Juliet
>Mark Antony and Cleopatra
>Petruchio and Katharina
>Bassanio and Portia
>Benedick and Beatrice
>Troilus and Cressida
>Florizel and Perdita

The men are on the left and speak first. The women on the right, respond. Match up each couple and then identify them.

MEN

1. "Women are made to bear, and so are you."

2. "There's beggary in the love that can be reckoned."

3. "I am no pilot; yet, wert thou as far as that vast shore washt with the furthest sea, I would adventure for such merchandise."

4. " 'Confess,' and 'love,' had been the very sum of my confession: O happy torment, when my

WOMEN

A. "O, but, sir, your resolution cannot hold, when 'tis opposed, as it must be, by the power of the king: One of these two must be necessities. Which then will speak,—that you must change this purpose, or I my life."

B. "Away then! I am lock't in one of them: If you do love me, you will find me out."

C. "O heavens! you love me not."

torturer doth teach me answers for deliverance! But let me to my fortune and the caskets."

5. "But it is certain I am loved of all ladies, only you excepted: and I would I could find it in my heart that I had not a hard heart; for, truly, I love none."

6. "Alas, a kind of godly jealousy—which, I beseech you, call a virtuous sin—makes me afeard."

7. "Apprehend nothing but jollity. The gods themselves, humbling their deities to love, have taken the shapes of beasts upon them: Jupiter became a bull, and bellowed; the green Neptune a ram, and bleated; and the fire-robed god, Golden Apollo, a poor humble swain, as I seem now: —their transformations were never for a piece of beauty rarer,—nor in a way so chaste, since my desires run not before mine honour, nor my lusts burn hotter than my faith."

D. "No such jade as you, if me you mean."

E. "I'll set a bourn how far to be beloved. Then must thou needs find out new heaven, new earth."

F. "Thou know'st the mask of night is on my face, else would a maiden blush depaint my cheek for that which thou hast heard me speak tonight. Fain would I dwell of form, fain deny what I have spoke: but farewell compliment! Dost thou love me?"

G. "A dear happiness to women: they would else have been troubled with a pernicious suitor. I thank God and my cold blood, I am of your humour for that: I had rather hear my dog bark at a crow than a man swear he loves me."

G A M E

8

What employment have we here?

HERE AT Shakespeare's Employment Agency, you have to choose the one job description written by the Bard. The other two comments about each job are from other writers.

Bonus Points: 5 points each for naming the Shakespearean speaker and the play; 10 points for identifying the authors of the other quotes.

ARCHER
1. "O! many a shaft at random sent finds mark the archer little meant."
2. "A well-experienced archer hits the mark his eye doth level at."
3. "The poet is like the prince of the clouds who haunts the tempest and laughs at the archer."

COOK
1. "Epicurean cooks sharpen with cloyless sauce his appetite."
2. "The cook was a good cook, as cooks go; and as cooks go she went."
3. "Cookery is become an art, a noble science; cooks are gentlemen."

MERCHANT
1. "Merchants have no country. The mere spot they stand on does not constitute so strong an attachment as that from which they draw their gains."
2. "Now I play a merchant's part, and venture madly on a

desperate mart."

  3. "I asked no other thing—no other—was denied—I offered Being—for it—the Mighty Merchant sneered."

SOLDIER

  1. "The most vital quality a soldier can possess is self-confidence, utter, complete and bumptious."
  2. "The first who was king was a fortunate soldier: Who serves his country well has no need of ancestors."
  3. "Why, old soldier, wilt thou undo the worth thou art unpaid for?"

ARCHITECT

  1. "Every man is the architect of his own fortune."
  2. "The fate of the architect is the strangest of all. How often he expends his whole soul, his whole heart and passion, to produce buildings into which he himself may never enter."
  3. "Chief architect and plotter of these woes."

TEACHER

  1. "The true teacher will have no disciple."
  2. "The schoolmaster is exceeding fantastical."
  3. "Let schoolmasters puzzle their brain, with grammar, and nonsense, and learning; good liquor, I stoutly maintain, gives genius a better discerning."

DOCTOR

  1. "By medicine life may be prolonged, yet death will seize the doctor too."
  2. "God heals and the doctor takes the fee."
  3. "Physicians mend or end us; but though in health we sneer, when sick we call them to attend us, without the least propensity to jeer."

BUTCHER

  1. "His father was a butcher, and I have been told heretofore by some of the neighbors, that when he was a boy he exercised his father's trade, but when he killed a calf he would do it in a high style and make a speech."

2. "Hog butcher for the world."

   3. "The lamb entreats the butcher."

LAWYER
   1. "Lawyers on opposite sides of a case are like the two parts of shears; they cut what comes between them, but not each other."

   2. "The first thing we do, let's kill all the lawyers."

   3. "It is not, what a lawyer tells me I may do; but what humanity, reason and justice, tell me I ought to do."

CLERK
   1. "All clerks, I mean the learned ones, in Christian kingdoms have their free voices."

   2. "A clerk foredoom'd his father's soul to cross, who pens a stanza when he should engross?"

   3. "When you send a clerk on business to a distant province, a man of rigid morals is not your best choice."

ACTOR
   1. "It is better to be making the news than taking it; to be an actor rather than a critic."

   2. "Most dear actors, eat no onions nor garlic, for we are to utter sweet breath."

   3. "The dream is the theater where the dreamer is at once scene, actor, prompter, stage manager, author, audience and critic."

WRITER
   1. "It is only a moment here and a moment there that the greatest writer has."

   2. "He writes very well for a gentleman."

   3. "Scribes, bards, poets, cannot think, speak, cast, write, sing."

G A M E

9

Mine enemies

SET THESE enemies to clashing again:
Hamlet and Laertes
Macbeth and Macduff
Tybalt and Mercutio
Hotspur and Prince Henry
Edgar and Edmund
Thurio and Valentine
Duke of Cornwall and Earl of Gloucester

The first speaker is in the left-hand column; his enemy answers on the right. Match each pair of opponents and then identify them.

FIRST SPEAKER

1. "Of all men else I have avoided thee: But get thee back; my soul is too much charged with blood of thine already."

2. "I'll play this bout first; set it by awhile.—Come—Another hit; what say you?"

3. "Follow me close, for I will speak to them.—Gentlemen, good den; a word with one of you."

4. "Fellows, hold the

ENEMY

A. "He that will think to live till he be old, give me some help!—O cruel!—O you gods!"

B. "I know it well, sir; you have an exchequer of words, and, I think, no other treasure to give your followers,—for it appears, by their bare liveries, that they live by your bare words."

C. "I'll make it greater ere I part from thee; and all the budding honours of

chair.—Upon these eyes of thine I'll set my foot."

5. "Sir, if you spend word for word with me, I shall make your wit bankrupt."

6. "For the hour is come to end the one of us; and would to God thy name in arms were now as great as mine!"

7. "Draw thy sword, if my speech offend a noble heart, thy arm may do thee justice: here is mine. Behold it is the privilege of mine honours, my oath, and my profession: I protest,—maugre thy strength, youth, place, and eminence, despite thy victor sword and fire-new fortune, thy valour and thy heart,—thou art a traitor; false to thy gods, thy brother, and thy father; conspirant 'gainst this high illustrious prince; and, from the extremest upward of thy head to the descent and dust below thy foot, a most toad-spotted traitor. Say thou 'no,' this sword, this arm, and my best spirits are bent, to prove upon thy heart, whereto I speak, thou liest."

thy crest I'll crop, to make a garland for my head."

D. "In wisdom I should ask thy name; but, since thy outside looks so fair and warlike, and that thy tongue some say of breeding breathes, what safe and nicely I might well delay by rule of knighthood, I disdain and spurn: Back do I toss these treasons to thy head; with the hell-hated lie o'erwhelm thy heart; which,—for they yet glance by, and scarcely bruise,—this sword of mine shall give them instant way, where they shall rest for ever.— Trumpets, speak!"

E. "And but one word with one of us? Couple it with something; make it a word and a blow."

F. "I have no words,—my voice is my sword; thou bloodier villain than terms can give thee out!"

G. "A touch, a touch, I do confess."

G A M E
10
Merely players

PICK THE actors who have performed in Shakespeare's plays.

1. Which actress starred as Hamlet in London?
- a. Faye Dunaway
- b. Sarah Bernhardt
- c. Lillian Gish
- d. Julie Christie

2. Which famous writer played Justice Shallow in *The Merry Wives of Windsor*?
- a. Norman Mailer
- b. George Bernard Shaw
- c. Oscar Wilde
- d. Charles Dickens

3. Which actor played Marcus Antonius in the 1952 movie of *Julius Caesar*?
- a. Marlon Brando
- b. Karl Malden
- c. Richard Burton
- d. Phil Silvers

4. Which child actor starred as Hamlet, Macbeth, Romeo, and Richard III?
- a. Freddy Bartholomew
- b. Mickey Rooney
- c. Master William Betty
- d. Jackie Coogan

5. Which comedian played Elvis Presley performing Hamlet?
- a. Woody Allen
- b. John Belushi
- c. Martin Mull
- d. Steve Martin

G A M E
11
Cakes and ale

To order dinner at The Shakespearean Inn, select the items on the menu that have been described by the Bard. There are at least two Shakespearean offerings in each category. Other dishes and drinks are provided by a selection of other writers.

Bonus Points: 5 points each for naming the Shakespearean speaker and the play; 10 points for identifying the authors of the other quotes.

APPETIZER
1. "The world's mine oyster, which I with sword will open."
2. "Neither fish nor flesh, nor good red herring."
3. "Then am I a shotten herring."
4. "She was the sweet-marjoram of the salad, or rather, the herb of grace."
5. "It's certain that fine women eat a crazy salad with their meat."

ENTREE
1. "Here's a pretty kettle of fish!"
2. "I will henceforth eat no fish of fortune's buttering."
3. "This Bouillabaisse a noble dish is—a sort of soup, or broth, or brew."
4. "When mighty roast beef was the Englishman's food, it ennobled our hearts, and enriched our blood, our soldiers were brave and our courtiers were good. Oh! the roast beef of old England!"
5. "If you give me any conserves, give me conserves of beef."

6. "A tale without love is like beef without mustard: an insipid dish."
7. "What say you to a piece of beef and mustard—a dish that I do love."
8. "You would eat the chickens in the shell."
9. "And we meet, with champagne and a chicken, at last."
10. "I want there to be no peasant in my realm so poor that he will not have a chicken in his pot every Sunday."
11. "They have a plentiful lack of wit, together with most weak hams."
12. "The capon burns, the pig falls from the spit."

SIDE DISH
1. "A gammon of bacon and two razes of ginger."
2. "What a world of gammon and spinach it is, though, ain't it!"
3. "No sheep, sweet lamb, unless we feed on your lips."
4. "A cup of Madeira and a cold capon's leg."
5. "Then a sentimental passion of a vegetable fashion must excite your languid spleen."
6. "Peas and beans are as dank here as a dog."

BREAD AND CHEESE
1. "Nobody, my darling, could call me a fussy man—but I do like a little bit of butter to my bread!"
2. "Gets him to rest, crammed with distressful bread."
3. "I speak this in hunger for bread, not in thirst for revenge."
4. "The people that once bestowed commands, consulships, legions, and all else, now concerns itself no more, and longs eagerly for just two things—bread and circuses!"
5. "The time-honored bread sauce of the happy ending."
6. "He would mouth with a beggar, though she smelt brown bread and garlic."
7. " 'Tis time I were choked with a piece of toasted cheese."
8. "The best of all physicians is apple pie and cheese."
9. "A dessert without cheese is like a beautiful woman with only one eye."

10. "I will make an end of my dinner; there's pippins and cheese to come."

BEER AND WINE

1. "A pot of good double beer, neighbour: drink and fear not."
2. "When the hoary Sage replied, 'Come, my lad, and drink some beer.'"
3. "Life isn't all beer and skittles, but beer and skittles, or something better of the same sort, must form a good part of every Englishman's education."
4. "Doth it not show vilely in me to desire small beer?"
5. "Ale, man, ale's the stuff to drink for fellows whom it hurts to think."
6. "For a quart of ale is a dish for a king."
7. "That's a marvellous searching wine."
8. "I cried for madder music and for stronger wine."
9. "I tasted—careless—then—I did not know the Wine came once a World—Did you?"
10. "A cup of wine that's brisk and fine."

DESSERT

1. "What calls back the past, like the rich pumpkin pie?"
2. "It is a paltry cap, a custard-coffin, a bauble, a silken pie."
3. "He lives upon mouldy stewed prunes and dried cakes."
4. "I ate 'umble pie with an appetite."
5. "Let him see to the substance of his cake instead of decorating with sugarplums."
6. "It's food too fine for angels; yet come, take and eat thy fill! It's Heaven's sugar cake."
7. "He that will have a cake out of the wheat must tarry the grinding."
8. "Honesty coupled to beauty is to have honey a sauce to sugar."

BEVERAGE

1. "One sweet word with thee.—Honey, and milk, and sugar."

2. "Things are seldom what they seem, skim milk masquerades as cream."
3. "For moving such a dish of skim milk with so honourable an action."
4. "Look here, Steward, if this is coffee, I want tea; but if this is tea, then I wish coffee."
5. "Tea, although an Oriental, is a gentleman at least; cocoa is a cad and coward, cocoa is a vulgar beast."
6. "Complacencies of the peignoir, and late coffee and oranges in a sunny chair."
7. "Should I, after tea and cakes and ices, have the strength to force the moment to its crisis?"

A notorious brothel in Paris Garden, Southwark. From Nicholas Goodman, *Holland's Leaguer* (1632).

GRAPHIC GAME
2
Seek thy fortune

STARTING at the arrow, follow the quotes through the maze on pages 28-29.

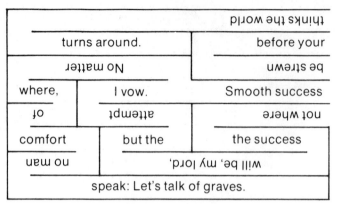

thinks the world

turns around. | before your

No matter | be strewn

where, | I vow. | Smooth success

of | attempt | not where

comfort | but the | the success

no man | will be, my lord,

speak: Let's talk of graves.

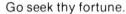

Go seek thy fortune.

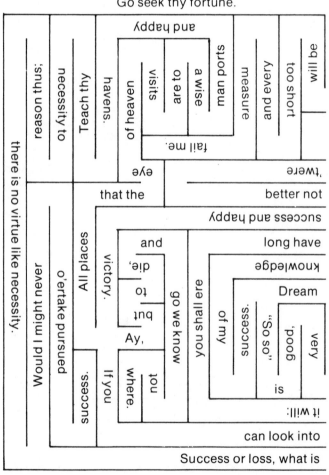

there is no virtue like necessity.

reason thus;

necessity to

Teach thy

havens.

of heaven

visits | are to | a wise | man ports

measure | and every

too short | will be

and happy

fail me.

eye | 'twere

that the | better not

success and happy

All places | and | long have

victory. | die, | knowledge

to | Dream

but | go we know | of my

Ay, | success. | "So so"

where. | good | very

you shall ere

Would I might never | If you | not

o'ertake pursued | is

success. | it will:

can look into

Success or loss, what is

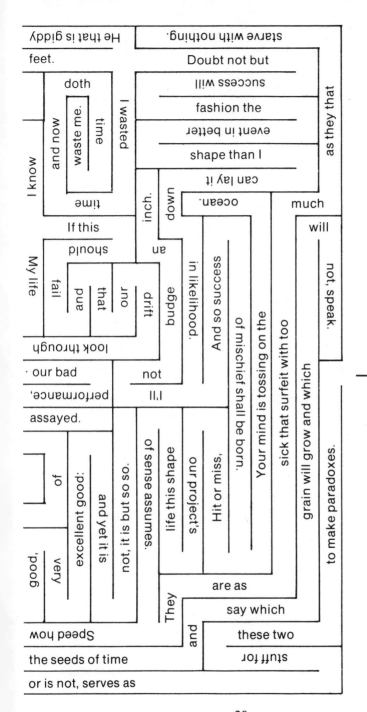

G A M E
12
To steal their brains

CHOOSE the works of literature upon which Shakespeare based some of his plays.

1. Which epic poem was the basis of *Troilus and Cressida*?
    a. *The Odyssey*   c. *Lysistrata*
    b. *The Iliad*   d. *The Way of Lao Tzu*

2. Which collection of stories was the source of *All's Well That Ends Well*?
    a. *The Canterbury Tales*   c. *Le Morte d'Arthur*
    b. *Gargantua*   d. *The Decameron*

3. Upon whose biographical works was *Julius Caesar* based?
    a. Plutarch   c. Sophocles
    b. Plato   d. Ovid

4. Which romantic story was the source for *As You Like It*?
    a. *The Lady of the Lake* by Sir Walter Scott
    b. *Don Quixote* by Miguel de Cervantes
    c. *Rosalynde* by Thomas Lodge
    d. *The Faerie Queene* by Edmund Spenser

5. Which prose romance provided the Gloucester subplot for *King Lear*?
    a. *Mother Bombie* by John Lyly
    b. *Tamburlaine the Great* by Christopher Marlowe
    c. *The Arcadia* by Sir Philip Sidney
    d. *Paradise Lost* by John Milton

G A M E
13
Fool's play

SHAKESPEARE must have loved fools; he made so many of them. In the following exchanges, match the fools with their foils:

Parolles and the Clown from *All's Well That Ends Well*
Proteus and Julia from *The Two Gentlemen of Verona*
Biron and Rosaline from *Love's Labour's Lost*
Launcelot and Lorenzo from *The Merchant of Venice*
Touchstone and Rosalind from *As You Like It*
Sir Andrew Aguecheek and the Clown from *Twelfth Night*
Achilles and Thersites from *Troilus and Cressida*
Caphis and Apemantus from *Timon of Athens*
Varro's Servant and the Fool from *Timon of Athens*
Lear and the Fool from *King Lear*
Earl of Kent and the Fool (twice) from *King Lear*

The straightmen speak first from the left-hand column; the fools zing them from the right. Match each couple and then identify them.

STRAIGHTMEN
1. "Where's the fool now?"

2. "Dost thou call me fool, boy?"

3. "Go to, thou art a witty fool; I have found thee."

4. "Begin, fool: it begins,

FOOLS
A. "How every fool can play upon the word!"

B. "The hour that fools should ask."

C. "Not i' the stocks, fool."

D. "All other titles thou hast given away."

'Hold thy peace.' "

5. "That you are well derived."

6. "This is nothing, fool."

7. "Thou art not altogether a fool."

8. "What time o' day?"

9. "Holla, you clown!"

10. "Peace, fool!"

11. "It is much that the Moor should be more than reason: but if she be less than an honest woman, she is indeed more than I took her for."

12. "Where learned you this, fool?"

E. "Did you find me in yourself, sir?"

F. "True; from a gentleman to a fool."

G. "I would have peace and quietness, but the fool will not."

H. "Peace, fool: he's not thy kinsman."

I. "I shall never begin, if I hold my peace."

J. "He last askt the question."

K. "Then 'tis like the breath of an unfee'd lawyer,— you gave me nothing for't."

L. "Nor thou altogether a wise man."

GAME

14

Strange bedfellows

WHAT WE know for sure about Shakespeare's life could fill a book—a matchbook. Use the most widely accepted theories about the often puzzling facts of his life when answering the questions.

Bonus Points: 5 points for devising an alternative theory for any of the questions; 10 points for convincing someone else of your theory.

1. As a struggling young playwright, Shakespeare must have done what most struggling young playwrights do: work at any job he could find. Shakespearean scholars have claimed that the Bard wrote so accurately about so many professions because he had worked in them before becoming a successful playwright. Which of the following professions have the scholars assigned to Shakespeare's resume?

a. page boy	f. captain in the Lancers
b. governor	g. soldier of fortune
c. butcher	h. schoolmaster
d. innkeeper	i. groom
e. accountant	j. lawyer's clerk

2. Why did Shakespeare, in his will, leave his wife his "second best bed"?

    a. To insult her.

    b. It was the custom in Elizabethan times to bury a wealthy man in the best bed.

    c. It was the custom to reserve the best bed for guests. Therefore, if Shakespeare had left his wife the best bed, it would have implied that she was only a guest in his house.

d. The best bed was given to the National Museum as part of its Shakespeare exhibit.

e. The best bed was being used in a production of *Macbeth.*

3. If Shakespeare didn't write Shakespeare, who did? According to various scholars, many of the following people wrote the plays. Name them.

a. Sir Walter Raleigh
b. Queen Elizabeth
c. Mary, Queen of Scots
d. Miguel de Cervantes
e. Ben Jonson

f. François Rabelais
g. Cardinal Wolsey
h. John Donne
i. John Milton
j. Martin Luther

4. Which one of these psychiatrists did not believe Shakespeare wrote the plays?

a. Sigmund Freud
b. Carl Jung
c. Havelock Ellis
d. Bob Hartley

5. In which book was it first suggested that Shakespeare was not the author of the plays?

a. *Volpone* by Ben Jonson
b. *The Vanity of Human Wishes* by Samuel Johnson
c. *Tom Sawyer* by Mark Twain
d. *The Romance of Yachting* by Colonel Joseph Hart
e. *Oliver Twist* by Charles Dickens

6. Some scholars claim that Shakespeare was a juvenile delinquent. Which of the following crimes have the professors recorded on his rap sheet?

a. pickpocket
b. public drunk
c. highwayman
d. forger
e. plagiarist
f. grave robber
g. deer poacher
h. rabbit poacher
i. con man
j. card cheat

7. The puzzle of the "Dark Lady of the Sonnets" has challenged scholars and gossip columnists through the ages. Which of the following possible "Dark Ladies" have been linked with Shakespeare?

a. Mary, Queen of Scots
b. Shakespeare's housekeeper
c. A negress
d. Queen Elizabeth
e. Ophelia
f. Lady Macbeth
g. The mistress of the owner of the Globe Theatre
h. The mistress of the Earl of Southampton
i. Lady Montague
j. Emilia Bassana

8. What geographical error did Shakespeare commit in *The Winter's Tale*?

a. He placed Scotland south of London.
b. He attributed a seacoast to Bohemia.
c. He attributed a desert to Bosnia-Herzegovina.
d. He called Moscow the capital of Poland.

G A M E
15
A caldron boiling

DOUBLE TOIL, double trouble, fire won't burn, caldron won't bubble—unless you can help the Three Witches from *Macbeth* get their ingredients straight. Match the magic part with its source.

PORTION	*POTION*
1. Sting	A. of newt
2. Wing	B. of hemlock
3. Lips	C. of salt-sea shark
4. Tooth	D. howlet's
5. Scale	E. of frog
6. Tongue	F. of dragon
7. Toe	G. of goat
8. Gall	H. of Turk
9. Slips	I. of blaspheming Jew
10. Eye	J. Tartar's
11. Nose	K. of birth-strangled babe
12. Finger	L. adder's
13. Leg	M. of wolf
14. Fork	N. of dog
15. Root	O. of yew
16. Liver	P. lizard's
17. Wool	Q. of bat
18. Fillet	R. of a fenny snake
19. Maw and gulf	S. blind-worm's

G A M E
16
Garden sport

WHAT STRANGE flowers must have grown in Shakespeare's garden! To pick those flowers, plants, herbs, and weeds, choose the lines written by Shakespeare. Other vegetation was grown by a variety of authors.

Bonus Points: 5 points for naming the Shakespearean speaker and the play; 10 points for identifying the authors of the other quotes.

1. "Our bodies are gardens; to the which our wills are gardeners: So that if we will plant nettles, or sow lettuce; set hyssop, and weed-up thyme; supply it with one gender of herbs, or distract it with many; either to have it sterile with idleness, or manured with industry; why, the power and corrigible authority of this lies in our wills."

2. "Knowst thou the land where the lemon trees bloom, where the gold orange glows in the deep thicket's gloom, where a wind ever soft from the blue heavens blows, and the groves are of laurel and myrtle and rose?"

3. "Gather the Rose of love, whilst yet is time."

4. "Gather ye rosebuds while ye may."

5. "Here's flowers for you: hot lavender, mints, savory, marjoram; the marigold, that goes to bed with the sun, and with him rises weeping; these are flowers of middle summer, and, I think, they are given to men of middle age."

6. "I know a little garden close, set thick with lily and red

rose, where I would wander if I might from dewy morn to dewy night."

7. "There's rosemary, that's for remembrance; pray you, love, remember: and there is pansies, that's for thoughts."

8. "To gild refined gold, to paint the lily, to throw a perfume on the violet."

9. "Rose is a rose is a rose is a rose."

10. "We have the receipt of fern-seed, we walk invisible."

11. "And the night climbing sucking the green from the ferns by these Berkshire boulders!"

12. "Thou art an elm, my husband,—I a vine, whose weakness, married to thy stronger state, makes me with thy strength to communicate: If aught possess thee from me, it is dross, usurping ivy, brier, or idle moss; who, all for want of pruning, with intrusion infect thy sap, and live on thy confusion."

13. "All their elves, for fear, creep into acorn-cups, and hide them there."

14. "The camomile, the more it is trodden on, the faster it grows."

15. " 'Long about knee-deep in June, 'bout the time strawberries melts on the vine."

16. "I saw good strawberries in your garden there."

17. "I knew a wench married in an afternoon as she went to the garden for parsley to stuff a rabbit."

18. "Just where one scarlet lily flamed I saw His footprint in the sod."

19. "I'll set a bank of rue, sour herb of grace."

20. "The grapes of wrath have not yet yielded all their bitter vintage."

21. "Our sea-walled garden, the whole land is full of weeds; her fairest flowers choked up, her fruit-trees all unprun'd, her hedges ruin'd."

22. "These criteria can be applied to people's words and actions to determine whether they are fragrant flowers or poisonous weeds."

23. "I am sleepy, and the oozy weeds about me twist."

24. "Nothing but thunder! Merciful Heaven, thou rather with thy sharp and sulphurous bolt splitt'st the unwedgeable and gnarled oak than the soft myrtle."

25. "Of all the trees that grow so fair, Old England to adorn, greater are none beneath the Sun than oak, and ash, and thorn."

A satyr.
From Jacopo Caviceo, *Libro del peregrino* (1526).

G A M E
17
All's well that ends well

PART OF Shakespeare's greatness was that he could speak with so many voices. The Bard could argue poetically for or against any proposition, and sometimes sideways. In this game, you're given the first part of a speech from one of the plays. Choose the correct second part of the quote.

1. "One touch of nature...
   a. hast robbed me of my youth!" (Hotspur, *King Henry the Fourth, Part One*)
   b. swells a man; and what a thing should I have been when I had been swelled!" (Sir John Falstaff, *The Merry Wives of Windsor*)
   c. makes the whole world kin." (Ulysses, *Troilus and Cressida*)
   d. shall be as strong as any man's in the disposing of new dignities." (Cassius, *Julius Caesar*)
   e. grieves me; and the spirit of my father, which I think is within me, begins to mutiny against this servitude: I will no longer endure it, though yet I know no wise remedy how to avoid it." (Orlando, *As You Like It*)

2. "I have set my life upon a cast...
   a. my pride fell with my fortunes." (Rosalind, *As You Like It*)
   b. Bait the hook well: this fish will bite." (Claudio, *Much Ado About Nothing*)
   c. play out the play." (Sir John Falstaff, *King Henry the Fourth, Part One*)
   d. and I will stand the hazard of the die." (King Richard,

King Richard the Third)

e. There was a star danced, and under that was I born."
(Beatrice, *Much Ado About Nothing*)

3. "I have done a thousand dreadful things...

    a. I'll note you in my book of memory." (Richard Plantagenet, *King Henry the Sixth, Part One*)

    b. as willingly as one would kill a fly." (Aaron, *Titus Andronicus*)

    c. By this leek, I will most horribly revenge. I eat and eat, I swear." (Pistol, *King Henry the Fifth*)

    d. I could brain him with his lady's fan." (Hotspur, *King Henry the Fourth, Part One*)

    e. I am falser than vows made in wine." (Rosalind, *As You Like It*)

4. "And do as adversaries do in war...

    a. Cry 'Havoc!' and let slip the dogs of war." (Marcus Antonius, *Julius Caesar*)

    b. sink or swim." (Hotspur, *King Henry the Fourth, Part One*)

    c. Give them great meals of beef and iron and steel, they will eat like wolves and fight like devils." (The Constable of France, *King Henry the Fifth*)

    d. press not a falling man too far." (Lord Chamberlain, *King Henry the Eighth*)

    e. strive mightily, but eat and drink as friends." (Tranio, *The Taming of the Shrew*)

5. "He jests at scars...

    a. he dies, and makes no sign." (King Henry, *King Henry the Sixth, Part Two*)

    b. I have more flesh than another man, and therefore more frailty." (Sir John Falstaff, *King Henry the Fourth, Part One*)

    c. lest too light winning make the prize light." (Prospero, *The Tempest*)

    d. that never felt a wound." (Romeo, *Romeo and Juliet*)

    e. Therefore think him as a serpent's egg which, hatched, would, as his kind, grow mischievous, and kill him in the shell." (Marcus Brutus, *Julius Caesar*)

6. "'Tis an ill cook...

    a. will make thee think thy swan a cow." (Mercutio, *Romeo and Juliet*)

    b. O flesh, flesh, how art thou fishified!" (Benvolio, *Romeo and Juliet*)

    c. that cannot lick his own fingers." (Second Serving Man, *Romeo and Juliet*)

    d. he was a man of an unbounded stomach." (Katharine, *King Henry the Eighth*)

    e. No man's pie is freed from his ambitious finger." (Duke of Buckingham, *King Henry the Eighth*)

7. "Things past redress...

    a. give thy thoughts no tongue." (Polonius, *Hamlet*)

    b. are now with me past care." (Duke of York, *King Richard the Third*)

    c. make us heirs of eternity." (King, *Love's Labour's Lost*)

    d. have a plentiful lack of wit." (Hamlet, *Hamlet*)

    e. be absolute for death." (Duke, *Measure for Measure*)

8. "Though she be but little...

    a. from the east to western Ind, no jewel is like Rosalind." (Rosalind [reading], *As You Like It*)

    b. she comes appareled like the spring." (Antiochus, *Pericles*)

    c. let every eye negotiate for itself and trust no agent." (Claudio, *Much Ado About Nothing*)

    d. fie, fie upon her! There's language in her eye, her cheek, her lip, nay, her foot speaks; her wanton spirits look out at every joint and motive of her body." (Ulysses, *Troilus and Cressida*)

    e. she is fierce." (Helena, *A Midsummer Night's Dream*)

9. "Why should a man, whose blood is warm within...

    a. sit like his grandsire, cut in alabaster." (Gratiano, *The Merchant of Venice*)

    b. let the end try the man." (Prince Henry, *King Henry the Fourth, Part Two*)

    c. hold you as a thing ensky'd and sainted." (Lucio, *Measure for Measure*)

    d. have a very poor and unhappy brains for drinking." (Cassio, *Othello*)

    e. bide the pelting of this pitiless storm, how shall your houseless heads and unfed sides, your loopt and window'd raggedness, defend you from seasons such as these?" (Lear, *King Lear*)

10. "Men have died from time to time, and worms have eaten them...

    a. but do not look for further recompense than thine own gladness that thou art employed." (Phebe, *As You Like It*)

    b. O, that this too too solid flesh would melt, thaw and resolve itself into a dew!" (Hamlet, *Hamlet*)

    c. What is a man if his chief good and market of his time be but to sleep and feed?" (Hamlet, *Hamlet*)

    d. but not for love." (Rosalind, *As You Like It*)

    e. The course of true love never did run smooth." (Lysander, *A Midsummer Night's Dream*)

G R A P H I C G A M E

3

Wherefore art thou?

HELP Juliet find her lover by following her speech through the maze on pages 44–45.

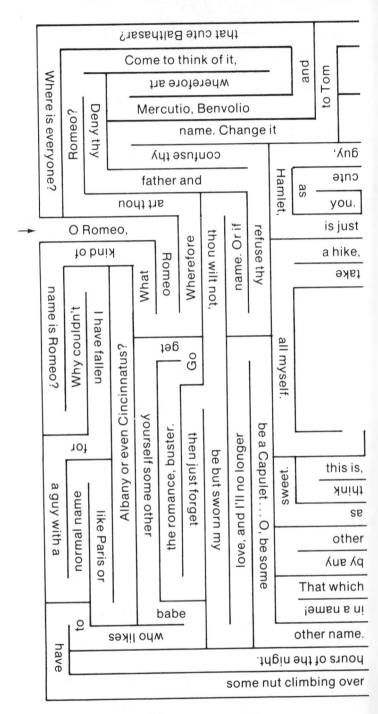

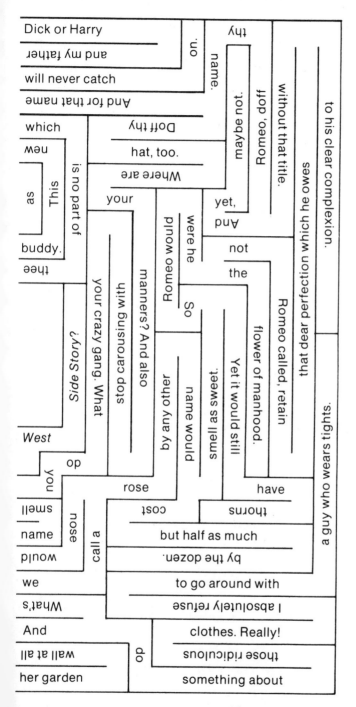

GAME
18

A rose by any other name

SHAKESPEARE was a prolific writer. Yet he still found time to provide generations of authors with titles for their books, plays, and movies. Without Shakespeare's help, William Faulkner might have written *The Noise and the Anger*.

In this game, you are given the speech from which a book, play, or movie title was taken. Choose that title.

1. *The Tempest*, Miranda: "O, wonder! How many goodly creatures are there here! How beauteous mankind is! O . . ."
- a. *Man, Proud Man* by Mabel Ulrich
- b. *Man and Superman* by George Bernard Shaw
- c. *Brave New World* by Aldous Huxley
- d. *Two Loves Have I* by Owen Pitman

2. *Twelfth Night*, Sir Toby Belch: "Out o'time, sir? ye lie.— Art any more than a steward? Dost thou think, because thou art virtuous, there shall be no more . . ."
- a. *Great Expectations* by Charles Dickens
- b. *Cakes and Ale* by W. S. Maugham
- c. *Daylight and Champagne* by G. M. Young
- d. *Rosemary for Remembrance* by M. R. Wilson

3. *Romeo and Juliet*, Romeo: "Courage, man; the hurt cannot be much." Mercutio: "No, 'tis . . ."
- a. *The Agony and the Ecstasy* by Irving Stone
- b. *In the Dark Backward* by H. W. Nevinson
- c. *Taken at the Flood* by D. Lambert
- d. *Not So Deep as a Well* by Dorothy Parker

4. *Hamlet,* Hamlet: "What a piece of work is man! how noble in reason! how infinite in faculty! in action..."
    a. *How Like a God* by Rex Stout
    b. *How Like an Angel* by A. G. MacDonnell
    c. *Men Are Not Gods* by G. B. Stern
    d. *Whistle Down the Wind* by Mary Hayley Bell

5. *Much Ado About Nothing,* Beatrice: "Speak, cousin; or, if you cannot, stop his mouth with a kiss, and let not him speak neither." Don Pedro: "In faith, lady, you have..."
    a. *The Merry Heart* by Frank Swinnerton
    b. *The Captive Heart* by Angus Macphail
    c. *A Majority of One* by Leonard Spiegelgass
    d. *The Man Who Came to Dinner* by George S. Kaufman

6. *The Tempest,* Trinculo: "Misery acquaints a man with..."
    a. *Mean Streets* by Martin Scorsese
    b. *The Digger's Game* by George V. Higgins
    c. *Strange Bedfellows* by Andrew Soutar
    d. *The Day of the Locust* by Nathanael West

7. *Romeo and Juliet,* Juliet: "Oh churl! drunk all, and left..."
    a. *The Big Sleep* by Raymond Chandler
    b. *No Friendly Drop* by Henry Wade
    c. *In Cold Blood* by Truman Capote
    d. *The Thin Man* by Dashiell Hammett

8. *King Lear,* Earl of Gloucester: "As flies to... are we to the gods, they kill us for their sport."
    a. *The Catcher in the Rye* by J. D. Salinger
    b. *The Naked and the Dead* by Norman Mailer
    c. *The Food of the Gods* by H. G. Wells
    d. *Wanton Boys* by Richard Oke

9. *Macbeth,* Macbeth: "I have no spur to prick the sides of my intent, but only..."
    a. *Vaulting Ambition* by Ellis Middleton

b. *Magnificent Obsession* by Lloyd C. Douglas
c. *An Affair to Remember* by Delmar Daves
d. *Brief Encounter* by Noel Coward

10. *The Taming of the Shrew,* Petruchio: "We will have rings, and things, and fine array; and..."
a. *Journey to the Center of the Earth* by Jules Verne
b. *The Boys in the Band* by Mart Crowley
c. *Kiss Me Kate* by Cole Porter
d. *Kiss Me Stupid* by Billy Wilder

11. *King John,* Bastard: "...shall not drive me back, when gold and silver becks me to come on."
a. *Guys and Dolls* by Damon Runyon
b. *The Once and Future King* by T. H. White
c. *Bell, Book and Candle* by John van Druten
d. *The Playboy of the Western World* by John Synge

12. Sonnet No. 29: "When in disgrace with...I all alone beweep my outcast state."
a. *Men, Women, and Dogs* by James Thurber
b. *The Ruling Class* by Peter Barnes
c. *The French Lieutenant's Woman* by John Fowles
d. *Fortune and Men's Eyes* by John Herbert

G A M E

19

A false creation

MAYBE Shakespeare wasn't such a great writer. Maybe he had a great editor. "This Shakespeare fellow," some quill-chewing editor may have said, "who does he think he is, Francis Bacon?"

In this game, some Shakespearean lines have been "unedited" so that each quote is close to, but not quite, as Shakespeare wrote it. In some sentences a word or two have been left out or added. In others, the word order or spelling has been changed to alter the sentence's meaning. Reedit these lines to read as Shakespeare wrote them.

Bonus Points: 5 points for identifying the play; 5 points for naming each speaker.

Example: Screw your courage to the sticky place.—Screw your courage to the *sticking* place. (Lady Macbeth, *Macbeth*)

1. There is a tide in the affairs of men which, taken at the ebb, leads on to misfortune.

2. Brevity is the soul of wit, drollery, jocularity, badinage and banter.

3. The empty vassal makes the greatest sound.

4. He that pays all debts dies.

5. Uneasy lies the head that wears a frown.

6. The evil that men do lives after them; the goods are oft interred with their bones.

7. Fight till the last grasp.

8. There is no virtue so simple but assumes some mark of vice on his outward parts.

9. A good mouth-filling roast.

10. He shows me where the bachelors sit, and there live we as weary as the day is long.

11. This is very midsummer gladness.

12. O, that men's lips should be to counsel deaf, but not to flattery!

The phoenix reborn from its funeral pyre.
From Geoffrey Whitney, *A Choice of Emblems* (1586).

GAME

20

The course of true love

Of LOVE, enough can never be said, although writers try.
In this game, a variety of authors try their hand at matching
Shakespeare in exaltations and denunciations of love. Choose
the Shakespearean love-lines.

Bonus Points: 5 points for naming each Shakespearean
speaker; 5 points for identifying the plays or sonnets; 10 points
for naming the writers of the other quotes.

1. "Love is a kind of warfare."

2. "Love is a devil: there is no evil angel but love."

3. "Ask me no reason why I love you; for though Love use
   Reason for his physician, he admits him not for his
   counsellor."

4. "Love and scandal are the best sweeteners of tea."

5. "I pray you, do not fall in love with me, for I am falser
   than vows made in wine."

6. "Stars that sweep, and turn, and fly, hear the Lovers'
   Litany: 'Love like ours can never die!'

7. "They that love beyond the world cannot be separated by
   it."

8. "In her first passion woman loves her lover, in all the
   others, all she loves is love."

9. "Love is not love which alters when it alteration finds."

10. "And ruin'd love, when it is built anew, grows fairer than

at first, more strong, far greater."

11. "Alas, that love, whose view is muffled still, should, without eyes, see pathways to his will."

12. "Love at the lips was touch as sweet as I could bear; and once that seemed too much; I lived on air."

13. "If ever thou shalt love, in the sweet pangs of it remember me."

14. "If you remember'st not the slightest folly that ever love did make thee run into, thou hast not loved."

15. "Is it, in Heav'n, a crime to love too well?"

16. "I love you more than words can wield the matter."

17. "The greater the love, the more false to its object, not to be born is the best for man; after the kiss comes the impulse to throttle, break the embraces, dance while you can."

18. "Four be the things I'd be better without: love, curiosity, freckles and doubt."

19. "And when I am o' horseback, I will swear I love thee infinitely."

20. "That Love is all there is, is all we know of Love."

G A M E
21
What's in a name?

FILL IN the blanks diagonally with the name of one of Shakespeare's characters, and you will also name five or six other characters reading across. The clues in parentheses help identify the diagonal character.

1. (A lover)

    __obin

    P__ins

    Ti__on

    Hel__n

    Luci__

2. (A schoolmaster)

    __aris

    C__nna

    He__ry

    Per__y

    Belc__

3. (A conspirator)

    __asset

    D__omio

    Gr__mio

    Pis__ol

    Rumo__r

    Jaque__

4. (A king)

    __udrey

    O__ivia

    Bl__unt

    Gur__ey

    Thai__a

    Angel__

G A M E

22

Quirky pens

UNDERLINE one word in each quote so that when you read the underlined words from top to bottom you have another Shakespearean quote.

Example:

A. "Good-morrow, carriers. <u>What's</u> o'clock?" (Gadshill, *King Henry the Fourth*)

B. "Come, go we <u>in</u> procession to the village." (King Henry, *King Henry the Fifth*)

C. "I am <u>a</u> poor friend of yours, that loves you." (Countess of Rousillon, *All's Well That Ends Well*)

D. "What is his <u>name</u>?" (Petruchio, *Taming of the Shrew*)

Answer: "What's in a name?" (Juliet, *Romeo and Juliet,* Act 2, Scene 2)

1. a. "That every nice offence should bear his comment." (Cassius, *Julius Caesar*)
   b. "For every inch of woman in the world." (Antigonus, *The Winter's Tale*)
   c. "He is a better scholar than I thought he was." (Mistress Page, *The Merry Wives of Windsor*)
   d. "What cares these roarers for the name of king?" (Boatswain, *The Tempest*)

2. a. "A most unnoble swerving." (Mark Antony, *Antony and Cleopatra*)
   b. "A plague upon this howling." (Boatswain, *The Tempest*)
   c. "This quarry cries on havoc." (Fortinbras, *Hamlet*)
   d. "Two households, both alike in dignity." (Chorus, *Romeo and Juliet*)

e. "You have receiv'd your griefs." (First Senator, *Timon of Athens*)

f. "If these be good people in a commonweal that do nothing but use their abuses in common houses." (Elbow, *Measure for Measure*)

3. a. "What a life dost thou lead!" (Prince Henry, *King Henry the Fourth, Part Two*)

b. "A horse cannot fetch, but only carry." (Launce, *The Two Gentlemen of Verona*)

c. " 'Tis not the trial of a woman's war." (Duke of Norfolk, *King Richard the Second*)

d. "For a hawk, a horse, or a husband." (Margaret, *Much Ado About Nothing*)

e. "By my troth, we that have good wits have much to answer for." (Touchstone, *As You Like It*)

f. "This will prove a brave kingdom to me." (Stephano, *The Tempest*)

g. "Hang her up for ever!" (Bawd, *Pericles*)

h. "I can keep honest counsel, ride, run, mar a curious tale in telling it." (Earl of Kent, *King Lear*)

i. "I pray you, stay not, but in haste to horse." (Bertram, *All's Well That Ends Well*)

4. a. "That very envy and the tongue of loss." (Duke of Illyria, *Twelfth Night*)

b. "And thereby for sealing the injury of tongues in courts and kingdoms." (Leontes, *The Winter's Tale*)

c. "What passion hangs these weights upon my tongue?" (Orlando, *As You Like It*)

d. "It may be his enemy is a gentleman of great sort." (King Henry, *King Henry the Fifth*)

e. "Your tale, sir, would cure deafness." (Miranda, *The Tempest*)

G A M E

23

Pun thee into shivers

EACH QUESTION suggests a dreadful pun based on the name of one of Shakespeare's characters. Name each character.

Bonus Points: 5 points for identifying the play each character appears in.

Example: Which weaver was not at the top of his trade? —Bottom, *A Midsummer Night's Dream.*

1. Which tavern hostess was always in a hurry?

2. Which duke could have been a state capital?

3. Which servant was also a rock 'n' roll star in the 1950s?

4. Which army commander could also clean up around the house?

5. Which constable could have been a noodle and a joint?

6. Which bishop was also an American President?

7. Which pet was a grouch?

8. Which French duke would be good over the rocks?

9. Which sheriff's officer could put the bite on thieves?

10. Which country justice was not too deep?

11. Who was the fastest servant?

12. Which hero was so noble they made him a capital of Europe?

13. Which constable was not very bright?

14. Which of Falstaff's companions was a hotshot?

15. Which doctor's servant was always getting kicked around?

A warrior's funeral.
From Olaus Magnus, *Historia de gentibus septentrionalibus* (1555).

GRAPHIC GAME
4
Set in order

STARTING at the arrow, follow the quotes through the maze on pages 58-59.

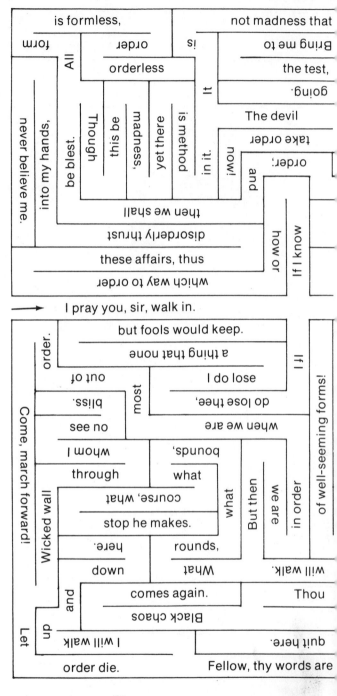

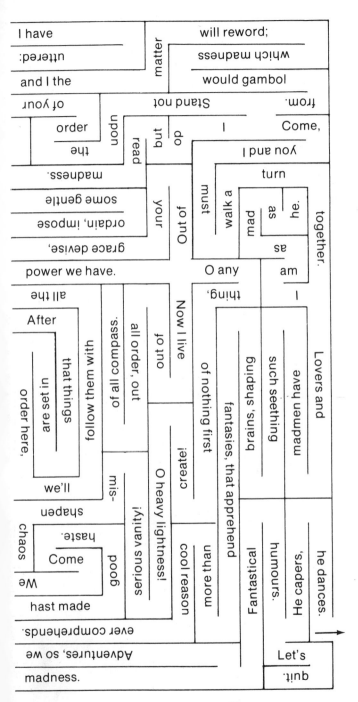

G A M E
24
A grievous fault

EACH OF these rewritten Shakespearean sonnets has a basic structural flaw. Although all of the Bard's words are there, they may be in the wrong order. Identify the cause of the disorder and rearrange the sonnet back into its original form.

1. Sonnet No. 53
   And you, but one, can every shadow lend,
   Since every one hath, every one, one shade.
   That millions of strange shadows on you tend,
   What is your substance, whereof are you made?
   And you in Grecian tires are painted new:
   On Helen's cheek all art of beauty set
   Is poorly imitated after you,
   Describe Adonis, and the counterfeit.
   And you in every blessed shape we know,
   The other as your bounty doth appear.
   The one doth shadow of your beauty show,
   Speak of the spring, and foison of the year.
   > But you like none, none you, for constant heart,
   > In all external grace you have some part.

2. Sonnet No. 14
   If from thyself to store thou wouldst convert,
   As truth and beauty shall together thrive;
   And, constant stars, in them I read such art,
   But from thine eyes my knowledge I derive;
   By oft predict that I in heaven find:

Or say with princes if it shall go well,
Pointing to each his thunder, rain, and wind;
Nor can I fortune to brief minutes tell;
Of plagues, of dearths, or seasons' quality;
But not to tell of good or evil luck.
And yet methinks I have astronomy;
Not from the stars do I my judgment pluck.
    Or else of thee this I prognosticate:
    Thy end is truth's and beauty's doom and date.

3. Sonnet No. 122
Full character'd with lasting brain,
Thy gift, thy tables, are within my memory.
Beyond all date, even to remain,
Which shall above that idle rank eternity.
Have faculty by nature to heart;
Or, at the least, so long as brain and subsist
Of thee, thy record never can be part
Till each to razed oblivion yield his mist.
Nor need I tallies thy dear love to hold,
That poor retention could not so much score;
To trust those tables that receive thee bold,
Therefore to give them from me was I more:
    Were to import forgetfulness in thee,
    To keep an adjunct to remember me.

G A M E
25
Impassioned confusion

WHAT PASSION can do to reason, actors can do to their lines. In these three impassioned speeches, the players have mangled the sentiments and the word order. All of Shakespeare's words are there; put the speeches back in their correct form.

1. *Macbeth,* Lady Macbeth:
"Out, damned time! fie, I call.—One, two; why, then, say 'tis murky to fear.—Power is blood.—Fie, my man, do't! A lord and afeard? What soldier knows it when we need none? Who can have our thought to account? Yet who would spot the old hell to have had so much out in him?"

2. *Julius Caesar,* Marcus Antonius:
"O, gentle me, with thou bleeding hand,
That I am meek and pardon the noblest man!
Thou art the ruins of these butchers
that lived in this piece of earth.
Woe to the tide of times
that ever shed the costly blood!"

3. *King Richard the Second,* John of Gaunt:
"This royal eden, this scepter'd throne of kings,
This earth of demi-Paradise, this seat of majesty,
This other isle, Mars;
This little world built by Nature for herself
Against infection, less happier lands, the silver sea, and
this happy breed of men;
This fortress set in this precious stone,

Which serves it in the office of a house,
Or as a moat defensive to a wall,
Against the envy of the hand of war;
This blessed earth, this realm, this England, this plot."

Fame.
From Henry Peacham, *Minerva Britanna* (1618).

G A M E

26

All the world's a stage

IN THIS game, you are given some famous speeches from the Bard's plays and the cue lines that precede those speeches. Match the cue with the speech.

Bonus Points: 5 points for naming the speaker or speakers; 5 points for naming the play.

CUES

1. "Shall I hear more, or shall I speak at this?"

2. "Light vanity, insatiate cormorant, consuming means, soon preys upon itself."

3. "He hath disgraced me, and hindered me half a million; laught at my losses, mockt at my gains, scorned my nation, thwarted my bargains, cooled my friends, heated mine enemies: and what's his reason?"

4. "Ay, so, God be wi' ye! Now I am alone."

5. "We must away; our wagon is prepared, and

SPEECHES

A. "This royal throne of kings, this scepter'd isle, this earth of majesty, this seat of Mars, this other Eden, demi-Paradise; this fortress built by Nature for herself against infection and the hand of war; this happy breed of men, this little world; this precious stone set in the silver sea, which serves it in the office of a wall, or as a moat defensive to a house, against the envy of less happier lands; this blessed plot, this earth, this realm, this England."

B. "The fault, dear Brutus, is not in our stars but in

time revives us:"

6. "These deeds must not be thought after these ways; so, it will make us mad."

7. "I will set down what comes from her, to satisfy my remembrance the more strongly."

8. "Thou seest we are not all alone unhappy: This wide and universal theatre presents more woeful pageants than the scene wherein we play in."

9. "What say'st thou to me now? Speak once again."

10. "Men at some time are masters of their fates:"

11. "Peace, ho! let us hear him."

12. "Rescue, fair lord, or else the day is lost!"

ourselves, that we are underlings."

C. "All the world's a stage, and all the men and women merely players: They have their exits and their entrances; and one man in his time plays many parts."

D. "Methought I heard a voice cry, *Sleep no more! Macbeth does murder sleep!*—the innocent sleep; sleep, that knits up the ravell'd sleave of care."

E. "A horse! a horse! my kingdom for a horse!"

F. "O what a rogue and peasant slave am I!"

G. "All's well that ends well: still the fine's the crown; whate'er the course, the end is renown."

H. "Out, damned spot! out, I say!—One, two; why, then 'tis time to do't.— Hell is murky!—Fie, my lord, fie! a soldier, and afeard? What need we fear who knows it, when none can call our power to account?—Yet who would have thought the old man to have had so much blood in him?"

I. "Beware the ides of March."

J. "Friends, Romans, countrymen, lend me your ears; I come to bury Caesar, not to praise him."

K. " 'Tis but thy name that is my enemy;—Thou art thyself though, not a Montague. What's Montague? it is nor hand, nor foot, nor arm, nor face, nor any other part belonging to a man. O, be some other name!

What's in a name? that which we call a rose by any other name would smell as sweet."

L. "I am a Jew. Hath not a Jew eyes? hath not a Jew hands, organs, dimensions, senses, affections, passions? fed with the same food, hurt with the same weapons, subject to the same diseases, heal'd by the same means, warm'd and cool'd by the same winter and summer, as a Christian? If you prick us, do we not bleed? if you tickle us, do we not laugh?"

G A M E
27
Wild talk

Two of the following three short scenes are as Shakespeare wrote them. The third scene was compiled by dice,
which took a random walk through all thirty-seven Shakespearean plays.

In a random walk, all movements are governed solely by
chance. Thus, I divided the plays into six groups and rolled a
single die to choose a group. I rolled the die again to choose a
play within that group; rolled again to choose an act within
that play, and once more to choose a scene within that act. I
rolled the die one final time to choose a speech within that
scene. Then I began the process all over again to choose a
second speech from anywhere within the thirty-seven plays
the dice wanted to go. In this random fashion, a scene was
chosen.

Pick the scene that was composed at random by the dice.

Bonus Points: 5 points for identifying the plays from which
the other two scenes were taken; 10 points each for identifying
the speakers in each of those plays; 20 points each for naming
the plays visited in the random walk; 25 points each for naming the speakers in those plays.

First Scene:
1. "Peace, my lord; hear, hear!"
2. "Shall's have a play of this? Thou scornful page, there lie
   thy part."
3. "O, gentlemen, help! Mine and your mistress!—O, my
   lord Posthumus! You ne'er kill'd Imogen till now:—help,
   help!—Mine honour'd lady!"
4. "Does the world go round?"

5. "How comes these staggers on me?"
6. "Wake, my mistress!"
7. "If this be so, the gods do mean to strike me to death with mortal joy."
8. "How fares my mistress?"
9. "O, get thee from my sight; thou gav'st me poison: dangerous fellow, hence! Breathe not where princes are!"

Second Scene
1. "Pr'ythee, peace."
2. "He receives comfort like cold porridge."
3. "The visitor will not give him o'er so."
4. "Look, he's winding up the watch of his wit; by and by it will strike."
5. "Sir,—"
6. "One:—tell."
7. "When every grief is entertain'd that's offer'd, comes to the entertainer—"
8. "A dollar."
9. "Dolour comes to him, indeed; you have spoken truer than you purposed."
10. "You have ta'en it wiselier than I meant you should."
11. "Therefore, my lord,—"
12. "Fie, what a spendthrift is he of his tongue!"

Third Scene
1. "Grace to boot! Of this make no conclusion, lest you say your queen and I are devils: yet, go on: Th' offences we have made you do, we'll answer; if you first sinned with us, and that with us you did continue fault, and that you slipt not with any but with us."
2. "Nay, it is petter yet:—give her this letter; for it is a omen that altogether's acquaintance with mistress Anne Page: and the letter is to desire and require her to solicit your master's desires to mistress Anne Page. I pray you, be gone; I will make an end of my dinner; there's pippins and cheese to come."

3. "O most unhappy strumpet!"
4. "Taurus—"
5. "Go, some of you convey him to the Tower."
6. "My kind Antonio, I can no other answer make, but thanks, and thanks, and ever; oft good turns are shuffled off with such uncurrent pay: But were my worth, as is my conscience, firm, you should find better dealing. What's to do? Shall we go see the reliques of this town?"
7. "Till noon! till night, my lord; and all night too."
8. "In most uneven and distracted manner. His actions show much like to madness: pray heaven his wisdom be not tainted! And why meet him at the gates, and redeliver our authorities there?"
9. "Mistrust it not; for, sure, Aeacides was Ajax,—called so from his grandfather."
10. "O perjured woman!—They are both forsworn: In this the madman justly chargeth them."
11. "He is a Roman; no more kin to me than I to your highness; who, being born your vassal, am something nearer."
12. "Look to the lady;—O, she's but overjoyed.—Early one blustering morn this lady was thrown upon this shore. I oped the coffin, found there rich jewels; recovered her, and placed her here in Diana's temple."
13. "For mine own part, I breathe free breath. I have seen the day of wrong through the little hole of discretion, and I will right myself like a soldier."
14. "Go, take their bodies hence."
15. "Ho, gentlemen! my lord calls."

G A M E
28
The seeming truth

FOR THIS game, the dice took a random walk through
Shakespeare's sonnets. To maintain a rhyming pattern, the dice
were asked to choose 3 quatrains and 1 couplet to compose a
random sonnet. Thus, there were 462 quatrains and 154
couplets for the dice to choose among at each throw. Some
interesting ideas can be generated if you give up the rhyme and
let the dice choose 14 lines from the 2,156 lines available.

Two of the sonnets below are as Shakespeare wrote them.
The third was randomly composed. Pick the random sonnet.

Bonus Points: 5 points each for guessing the numbers of the
two normal sonnets; 10 points each for guessing the sonnets to
which the three quatrains and the couplet of the random sonnet
normally belong.

1. But do thy worst to steal thyself away,
   For term of life thou art assured mine;
   And life no longer than thy love will stay,
   For it depends upon that love of thine.
   Then need I not to fear the worst of wrongs,
   When in the least of them my life hath end.
   I see a better state to me belongs
   Than that which on thy humour doth depend:
   Thou canst not vex me with inconstant mind,
   Since that my life on thy revolt doth lie.
   O, what a happy title do I find,
   Happy to have thy love, happy to die!
       But what's so blessed-fair that fears no blot?
       Thou mayst be false, and yet I know it not.

2. How can I, then, return in happy plight,
   That am debarr'd the benefit of rest?
   When day's oppression is not eas'd by night,
   But day by night, and night by day, oppress'd?
   To me, fair friend, you can never be old,
   For as you were when first your eye I ey'd,
   Such seems your beauty still. Three winters' cold
   Have from the forests shook three summers' pride;
   The painful warrior famoused for fight,
   After a thousand victories once foil'd,
   Is from the book of honour razed quite,
   And all the rest forgot for which he toil'd:
   > Thus have I had thee, as a dream doth flatter,
   > In sleep a king, but waking no such matter.

3. As a decrepit father takes delight
   To see his active child do deeds of youth,
   So I, made lame by Fortune's dearest spite,
   Take all my comfort of thy worth and truth;
   For whether beauty, birth, or wealth, or wit,
   Or any of these all, or all, or more,
   Entitled in their parts do crowned sit,
   I make my love engrafted to this store:
   So then I am not lame, poor, nor despis'd,
   Wilst that this shadow doth such substance give,
   That I in thy abundance am suffic'd,
   And by a part of all thy glory live.
   > Look what is best, that best I wish in thee;
   > This wish I have; then ten times happy me!

G A M E
29
Upon thy stars

THIS GAME was conceived by author and editor Charles Tips, who once hitchhiked from Texas to Ohio for a good Shakespearean argument.

In this game, you are given a speech that provides astrological clues to a character's identity, as well as a horoscope based on that character's life in the play. Choose the correct character by his forecast.

1. "My father named me..., who being, as I am, littered under Mercury, was likewise a snapper-up of unconsidered trifles."

Horoscope: With Mercury as your ruling planet, you have a happy, carefree nature, enjoy fine clothes and are often the life of the party. You have many talents that place you above the common man; singing would be a good career for you, as would retail sales. You are good with your hands and quick with your wits, but you may be too smart for your own good.
>   a. Balthazar, *The Comedy of Errors*
>   b. Autolycus, *The Winter's Tale*
>   c. Bottom, *A Midsummer Night's Dream*
>   d. Froth, *Measure for Measure*

2. "Thrice hath this..., Mars in swathling clothes, this infant warrior, in his enterprises discomfited great Douglas, ta'en him once, enlarged him, and made a friend of him, to fill the mouth of deep defiance up and shake the peace and safety of our throne."

Horoscope: Ruled by Mars, your hot temper may get you

into trouble. You will have great success in all your efforts, but will jealously guard the spoils of your victories. You live for danger, honor and glory, but your loyalty wavers because of your rebellious nature. You are too blunt with cautious friends, who may desert you in your time of need.

    a. Marcus Brutus, *Julius Caesar*
    b. Antony, *Antony and Cleopatra*
    c. Roderigo, *Othello*
    d. Hotspur, *King Henry the Fourth, Part One*

3. "Even or odd, of all days in the year come Lammas Eve at night shall she be fourteen."

Horoscope: A daughter of the sun, your heart is pure, but you will be surrounded by trouble in romance and family affairs. You have no taste for the trivial or insincere, and are resolute to your purpose in life. Your pride may get you into trouble with your elders, but you will make your own decisions and stick to them no matter what the consequences. Be careful with strong drink and sharp objects.

    a. Hero, *Much Ado About Nothing*
    b. Juliet, *Romeo and Juliet*
    c. Katharina, *The Taming of the Shrew*
    d. Lady Macbeth, *Macbeth*

4. "My father compounded with my mother under the dragon's tail, and my nativity was under Ursa Major, so that it follows, I am rough and lecherous.—Tut, I should have been that I am, had the maidenliest star in the firmament twinkled on my bastardizing."

Horoscope: Governed by Mars, your ambitious nature will carry you far in the affairs of state, despite your lowly beginnings. You can be affectionate and charming when it suits your purpose, but your wild jealousy may get the best of you. You have a talent for writing, but your self-destructive tendencies my lead to arm injuries. You will be very successful with the opposite sex, but romance will be subservient to your ambition. Lack of self-control may lead to treachery and homicidal rage, but your inner sense of justice will prevail in the end.

    a. Edmund, *King Lear*
    b. Titus, *Titus Andronicus*
    c. Richard, *King Richard the Third*
    d. Hector, *Troilus and Cressida*

5. "Our jovial star reigned at his birth, and in our temple was he married."

Horoscope: Ruled by Jupiter, you will do well in marriage and will travel, though not always voluntarily. You sometimes show strange choice in clothes. You display confidence in those you care for, but are too easily misguided by people with ulterior motives. You are a valiant fighter, though your services are not always appreciated. Persevere and have faith, for you will be reunited with the ones you love in the end.

    a. Parolles, *All's Well That Ends Well*
    b. Claudio, *Much Ado About Nothing*
    c. Posthumus, *Cymbeline*
    d. Polixenes, *The Winter's Tale*

Mars.
From Vincenzo Cartari, *Imagini de gli dei delli antichi* (1615).

G A M E
30
Finish the jest

EACH SPEECH in the following scene is the closing line from one of Shakespeare's plays. Name each speaker and the play.

1. "So, call the field to rest: and let's away, to part the glories of this happy day."

2. "Sound drums and trumpets;—and to London all: and more such days as these to us befall!"

3. "Sound drums and trumpets! farewell sour annoy! For here, I hope, begins our lasting joy."

4. "Rebellion in this land shall lose his sway, meeting the check of such another day: And since this business so fair is done, let us not leave till all our own be won."

5. "Go, bid the soldiers shoot."

6. "Set on there!—Never was a war did cease, ere bloody hands were wash'd, with such a peace."

7. "The words of Mercury are harsh after the songs of Apollo. You that way: we this way."

8. "Nay, then, thus:—we came into the world like brother and brother; and now let's go hand in hand, not one before another."

9. "Give me your hands, if we be friends, and Robin shall restore amends."

10. "I'll make a voyage to the Holy Land, to wash this blood off from my guilty hand:—March sadly after; grace my

75

mournings here, in weeping after this untimely bier."

11. "I have a motion much imports your good; whereto if you'll a willing ear incline, what's mine is yours, and what is yours is mine.—So, bring us to our palace; where we'll show what's yet behind, that's meet you all should know."

12. "Now I want spirits to enforce, art to enchant; and my ending is despair, unless I be relieved by prayer, which pierces so, that it assaults mercy itself, and frees all faults. As you from crimes would pardoned be, let your indulgence set me free."

13. "The weight of this sad time we must obey; speak what we feel, not what we ought to say. The oldest hath borne most: we that are young shall never see so much, nor live so long."

14. "A great while ago the world begun, with hey, ho, the wind and the rain:—But that's all one, our play is done, and we'll strive to please you every day."

15. "So, on your patience evermore attending, new joy wait on you! Here our play hath ending."

DOUBLE CROSTIC

1

Double, double

START BY answering any of the clues you can (each missing word is part of a Shakespearean quote). Then begin to fill in the diagram on page 81 by transferring each letter from the completed clues to the appropriately numbered box. As words begin to become clear in the diagram, experiment by transferring letters to unanswered clues (the small letter in the upper right-hand corner of each box corresponds to one of the clues).

When you have completed the diagram, you will have a speech by Benedick from *Much Ado About Nothing*.

CLUES

A. *Troilus and Cressida,* Thersites: "The plague of Greece upon thee, thou mongrel

$\overline{33}$ $\overline{6}$ $\overline{119}$ $\overline{186}$ $\overline{104}$ $\overline{13}$ $\overline{52}$ $\overline{123}$ $\overline{83}$ $\overline{20}$ lord!"

B. *King Henry the Sixth, Part Two,* King Henry: "The care you have of us, to $\overline{68}$ $\overline{27}$ $\overline{130}$ down thorns that would annoy our foot, is worthy praise."

C. *Love's Labour's Lost,* Sir Nathaniel: "Truly, Master

$\overline{45}$ $\overline{136}$ $\overline{107}$ $\overline{74}$ $\overline{36}$ $\overline{156}$ $\overline{195}$ $\overline{110}$ $\overline{59}$ $\overline{17}$, the epithets are sweetly varied, like a scholar at the least."

D. *Love's Labour's Lost,* King: "A man in all the world's new fashion planted, that hath a mint of

$\overline{5}$ $\overline{78}$ $\overline{67}$ $\overline{32}$ $\overline{152}$ $\overline{192}$ $\overline{125}$ in his brain."

77

E. *King Lear*, Duke of Albany: "You are not worth the dust which the $\overline{15}\ \overline{106}\ \overline{29}\ \overline{159}$ wind blows in your face."

F. *King Henry the Sixth, Part One*, Mayor of London: "I'll call for clubs, if you will not away:—this cardinal's more $\overline{197}\ \overline{96}\ \overline{132}\ \overline{93}\ \overline{37}\ \overline{72}\ \overline{25}$ than the devil."

G. *The Tempest*, Ferdinand: "Full many a lady I have eyed with best $\overline{84}\ \overline{42}\ \overline{204}\ \overline{71}\ \overline{24}\ \overline{165}$; and many a time the harmony of their tongues hath into bondage brought my too diligent ear."

H. *King John*, King John: "The $\overline{111}\ \overline{7}\ \overline{44}$ ribs of peace must by the hungry now be fed upon."

I. *The Two Gentlemen of Verona*, Speed: "You have learned . . . to watch, like one that fears robbing; to speak puling, like a beggar at $\overline{151}\ \overline{201}\ \overline{58}\ \overline{133}\ \overline{11}\ \overline{163}\ \overline{190}\ \overline{60}\ \overline{34}\ \overline{207}$."

J. *Antony and Cleopatra*, Mark Antony: "Come, let's all take hands, till that the conquering $\overline{26}\ \overline{129}\ \overline{202}\ \overline{53}$ hath steept our sense in soft and delicate Lethe."

K. *Troilus and Cressida*, Troilus: "Her $\overline{40}\ \overline{112}\ \overline{108}$ is India; there she lies, a pearl."

L. *The Winter's Tale*, Clown: "I must have saffron, to colour the warden pies, mace—dates,—none, that's out of my note; nutmegs, seven; a race or two of ginger; but that I may beg;—four pound of prunes, and as many of $\overline{64}\ \overline{139}\ \overline{56}\ \overline{76}\ \overline{35}\ \overline{160}\ \overline{101}$ o' the sun."

M. *Romeo and Juliet*, Romeo: "Love goes toward love, as schoolboys from their $\overline{191}\ \overline{87}\ \overline{162}\ \overline{8}\ \overline{51}$."

N. *King Henry the Sixth, Part One,* Duke of Alencon: "None but Samsons and Goliases it sendeth forth to skirmish. One to ten! Lean, $\overline{205}\ \overline{14}\ \overline{155}\ \overline{57}\ \overline{121}\ \overline{19}\ \overline{66}\ \overline{183}$ rascals! who would e'er suppose they had such courage and audacity?"

O. *A Midsummer Night's Dream,* Lysander: "And, which is more than all these boasts can be, I am beloved of beauteous $\overline{2}\ \overline{158}\ \overline{128}\ \overline{138}\ \overline{69}\ \overline{179}$."

P. *King Henry the Fifth,* King Henry: "Thus may we gather honey from the $\overline{82}\ \overline{23}\ \overline{196}\ \overline{161}$ and make a moral of the devil himself."

Q. *Julius Caesar,* Marcus Brutus: "But this same day must end that work the ides of March begun: and $\overline{46}\ \overline{62}\ \overline{185}\ \overline{31}\ \overline{143}\ \overline{103}\ \overline{55}$ we shall meet again I know not."

R. *The Merchant of Venice,* Shylock: "He rails, even there where merchants most do congregate, on me, my bargains, and my well-won $\overline{77}\ \overline{174}\ \overline{28}\ \overline{73}\ \overline{193}\ \overline{114}$."

S. *Troilus and Cressida,* Achilles: "Your last service was sufferance, 'twas not $\overline{22}\ \overline{131}\ \overline{88}\ \overline{149}\ \overline{12}\ \overline{115}\ \overline{18}\ \overline{41}\ \overline{142}$."

T. *King Richard the Second,* King Richard: "From under this $\overline{137}\ \overline{85}\ \overline{141}\ \overline{48}\ \overline{198}\ \overline{30}\ \overline{65}\ \overline{122}\ \overline{109}\ \overline{43}\ \overline{171}$ ball, he fires the proud tops of the eastern pines, and darts his light through every guilty hole."

U. *Romeo and Juliet,* Romeo: "My lips, two blushing pilgrims, ready stand to smooth that rough touch with a $\overline{187}\ \overline{99}\ \overline{75}\ \overline{134}\ \overline{164}\ \overline{200}$ kiss."

V. *Macbeth,* Macbeth: "Say from whence you owe this strange intelligence? or why upon this blasted

$\overline{124}\ \overline{81}\ \overline{50}\ \overline{173}\ \overline{181}$ you stop our way."

W. *All's Well That Ends Well,* Second Gentleman: "We met him $\overline{176}\ \overline{118}\ \overline{91}\ \overline{199}\ \overline{98}\ \overline{49}\ \overline{80}\ \overline{166}\ \overline{170}\ \overline{97}\ \overline{178}$; for thence we came, and, after some dispatch in hand at court, thither we bend again."

X. *The Comedy of Errors,* Antipholus of Syracuse: "Come, Dromio, come, these jests are out of

$\overline{9}\ \overline{63}\ \overline{127}\ \overline{203}\ \overline{116}\ \overline{92}$; reserve them till a merrier hour than this."

Y. *Macbeth,* Macbeth: "Why do I yield to that suggestion whose horrid image doth unfix my hair, and make my seated $\overline{188}\ \overline{206}\ \overline{175}\ \overline{54}\ \overline{126}$ knock at my ribs."

Z. *Much Ado About Nothing,* Leonato: "Their counsel turns to passion, which before would give preceptial medicine to rage, fetter strong madness in a silken _____."

$\overline{168}\ \overline{147}\ \overline{140}\ \overline{79}\ \overline{182}\ \overline{16}$.

Z1. *Measure for Measure,* Angelo: O place, O form, how often dost thou with thy case, thy habit, wrench awe from fools, and tie the wiser souls to thy false

$\overline{61}\ \overline{3}\ \overline{144}\ \overline{180}\ \overline{89}\ \overline{94}\ \overline{150}$!"

Z2. *Cymbeline,* Leonatus Posthumus: "I will remain the loyal'st husband that did e'er plight $\overline{208}\ \overline{157}\ \overline{194}\ \overline{117}\ \overline{169}$."

Z3. *King Henry the Sixth, Part One,* Countess of Auvergne: "This is a riddling merchant for the $\overline{70}\ \overline{105}\ \overline{120}\ \overline{113}\ \overline{21}$; he will be here and yet he is not here."

Z4. *A Midsummer Night's Dream,* Theseus: "Where I have come, great clerks have purposed to greet me with premeditated welcomes; where I have seen them

$\overline{1}\ \overline{153}\ \overline{189}\ \overline{90}\ \overline{38}\ \overline{100}$ and look pale."

Z5. *Twelfth Night,* Viola: "O, such love could be but recompensed, though you were crowned the

$\overline{135}\ \overline{148}\ \overline{86}\ \overline{10}\ \overline{177}\ \overline{39}\ \overline{47}\ \overline{167}\ \overline{184}$ of beauty!"

Z6. *King Lear,* Earl of Kent: "The gods to their dear

$\overline{4}\ \overline{102}\ \overline{154}\ \overline{172}\ \overline{146}\ \overline{95}\ \overline{145}$ take thee, maid, that justly think'st, and hast most rightly said!"

1 Z4	2 O	3 Z1		4 Z6	5 D	6 A	7 H	8 M	9 X		10 Z5	11 I	12 S	13 A	14 N	15 E
16 Z	17 C		18 S	19 N	20 A		21 Z3	22 S	23 P	24 G	25 F		26 J	27 B	28 R	29 E
	30 T	31 Q	32 D	33 A	34 I		35 L	36 C		37 F	38 Z4	39 Z5		40 K	41 S	42 G
43 T	44 H	45 C		46 Q	47 Z5	48 T	49 W		50 V	51 M		52 A	53 J	54 Y	55 Q	56 L
57 N	58 I	59 C		60 I	61 Z1		62 Q	63 X	64 L		65 T	66 N	67 D	68 B	69 O	70 Z3
71 G	72 F	73 R	74 C	75 U	76 L		77 R	78 D	79 Z	80 W	81 V		82 P	83 A	84 G	85 T
	86 Z5	87 M		88 S	89 Z1	90 Z4	91 W	92 X	93 F		94 Z1	95 Z6	96 F	97 W		98 W
99 U	100 Z4		101 L	102 Z6	103 Q		104 A	105 Z3	106 E	107 C	108 K		109 T	110 C	111 H	112 K
113 Z3	114 R		115 S	116 X		117 Z2	118 W	119 A		120 Z3	121 N	122 T	123 A	124 V		125 D
126 Y	127 X	128 O		129 J		130 B	131 S	132 F	133 I	134 U		135 Z5	136 C	137 T		138 O
139 L	140 Z	141 T	142 S		143 Q	144 Z1	145 Z6		146 Z6	147 Z	148 Z5	149 S	150 Z1	151 I		152 D
153 Z4	154 Z6		155 N	156 C	157 Z2	158 O		159 E	160 L	161 P	162 M	163 I	164 U	165 G		166 W
167 Z5	168 Z	169 Z2		170 W	171 T	172 Z6		173 V	174 R	175 Y	176 W		177 Z5	178 W	179 O	180 Z1
	181 V	182 Z	183 N		184 Z5	185 Q	186 A	187 U		188 Y	189 Z4	190 I		191 M	192 D	193 R
194 Z2	195 C	196 P		197 F	198 T		199 W	200 U	201 I	202 J	203 X	204 G	205 N	206 Y	207 I	208 Z2

DOUBLE CROSTIC

2

Toil and trouble

EACH CLUE is a Shakespearean quote with a word missing. Begin to solve the double crostic by filling in any of the missing words that you can. Then transfer each letter from the completed clues to the appropriately numbered box in the diagram on page 85. As words begin to take shape in the diagram, transfer letters back to unanswered clues. (The small letter in the upper right-hand corner of each box in the diagram tells you in which clue the letter belongs.)

When you have completely filled in the diagram, you will have a speech by Biron from *Love's Labour's Lost.*

CLUES

A. *King Henry the Fourth, Part One,* Hotspur: "Oft the teeming earth is with a kind of colic pincht and vext by the imprisoning of unruly wind within her womb; which, for enlargement striving, shakes the old

$\overline{132}$ $\overline{95}$ $\overline{76}$ $\overline{57}$ $\overline{88}$ $\overline{125}$ $\overline{11}$ earth."

B. *The Merry Wives of Windsor,* Simple: "I thank your worship: I shall make my master glad with these

$\overline{2}$ $\overline{85}$ $\overline{93}$ $\overline{38}$ $\overline{20}$ $\overline{22}$ $\overline{71}$."

C. *Hamlet,* Horatio: "The moist $\overline{1}$ $\overline{120}$ $\overline{52}$ $\overline{101}$, upon whose influence Neptune's empire stands, was sick almost to doomsday with eclipse."

D. *Much Ado About Nothing,* Friar Francis: "Doubt not but success will fashion the event in better shape than I can lay it down in $\overline{75}$ $\overline{119}$ $\overline{10}$ $\overline{47}$ $\overline{89}$ $\overline{59}$ $\overline{128}$ $\overline{24}$ $\overline{133}$ $\overline{4}$."

E. *Troilus and Cressida,* Thersites: "That $\overline{50}$ $\overline{12}$ $\overline{113}$ $\overline{39}$ $\overline{98}$ old mouse-eaten dry cheese, Nestor."

F. *Romeo and Juliet,* Friar Laurence: "The sweetest honey is loathsome in his own deliciousness, and in the

$\overline{36}$ $\overline{110}$ $\overline{62}$ $\overline{127}$ $\overline{56}$ confounds the appetite."

G. *King Henry the Sixth, Part One,* Earl of Suffolk: "When thou comest to kneel at Henry's feet, thou mayst

$\overline{44}$ $\overline{16}$ $\overline{118}$ $\overline{129}$ $\overline{78}$ $\overline{107}$ $\overline{14}$ him of his wits with wonder."

H. *King Henry the Fourth, Part Two,* Warwick: "There is a

$\overline{15}$ $\overline{26}$ $\overline{97}$ $\overline{60}$ $\overline{134}$ $\overline{53}$ $\overline{66}$ in all men's lives, figuring the nature of the times deceased."

I. *Macbeth,* Angus: "Now does he feel his title hang

$\overline{8}$ $\overline{68}$ $\overline{103}$ $\overline{72}$ $\overline{108}$ about him, like a giant's robe upon a dwarfish thief."

J. *King Richard the Third,* King Richard: "Give me a watch.—Saddle white $\overline{131}$ $\overline{64}$ $\overline{123}$ $\overline{130}$ $\overline{80}$ $\overline{5}$ for the field tomorrow."

K. *King Henry the Eighth,* Duke of Buckingham: "Charles the emperor, under pretence to see the queen his aunt,— for 'twas indeed his colour, but he came to whisper

$\overline{58}$ $\overline{117}$ $\overline{40}$ $\overline{30}$ $\overline{100}$ $\overline{121}$."

L. *All's Well That Ends Well,* King: "Here, take her hand, proud scornful boy, unworthy this good gift, that dost in vile misprision $\overline{29}$ $\overline{116}$ $\overline{17}$ $\overline{54}$ $\overline{135}$ $\overline{91}$ $\overline{112}$ up my love, and her desert."

M. *Measure for Measure,* Angelo: "My unsoil'd name, th' austereness of my life, my $\underline{}_{18}$ $\underline{}_{92}$ $\underline{}_{3}$ $\underline{}_{81}$ $\underline{}_{77}$ against you."

N. *Love's Labour's Lost,* Biron: "We are again forsworn, in will and error. Much upon this it is: and might not you forestall our sport to make us thus $\underline{}_{31}$ $\underline{}_{104}$ $\underline{}_{33}$ $\underline{}_{96}$ $\underline{}_{114}$ $\underline{}_{48}$?"

O. *Pericles,* Simonides: "Opinion's but a fool, that makes us $\underline{}_{111}$ $\underline{}_{65}$ $\underline{}_{106}$ $\underline{}_{83}$ the outward habit by the inward man."

P. *The Merchant of Venice,* Gratiano: A $\underline{}_{13}$ $\underline{}_{82}$ $\underline{}_{27}$ $\underline{}_{90}$ of gold, a paltry ring that she did give to me."

Q. *Macbeth,* Lady Macbeth: "Stop up th' access and passage to remorse, that no compunctious visitings of nature $\underline{}_{7}$ $\underline{}_{55}$ $\underline{}_{35}$ $\underline{}_{70}$ $\underline{}_{19}$ my fell purpose."

R. *Hamlet,* First Player: "Who this had seen, with tongue in $\underline{}_{99}$ $\underline{}_{45}$ $\underline{}_{41}$ $\underline{}_{69}$ $\underline{}_{73}$ steept, 'gainst Fortune's state would treason have pronounced."

S. *The Taming of the Shrew,* Petruchio: " ' $\underline{}_{84}$ $\underline{}_{102}$ $\underline{}_{63}$ $\underline{}_{105}$ told me you were rough, and coy, and sullen, and now I find report a very liar."

T. *As You Like It,* Rosalind: "I see no more in you than without candle may go dark to bed,—must you be therefore $\underline{}_{49}$ $\underline{}_{25}$ $\underline{}_{42}$ $\underline{}_{87}$ $\underline{}_{94}$ and pitiless?"

U. *Much Ado About Nothing,* Margaret: "And God keep him out of my sight when the dance is $\underline{}_{46}$ $\underline{}_{124}$ $\underline{}_{32}$ $\underline{}_{51}$!"

V. *King Richard the Third,* Messenger: "If presently you will take horse with him, and with all speed post with him toward the north, to $\overline{136}\ \overline{61}\ \overline{28}\ \overline{86}$ the danger that his soul divines."

W. *The Merry Wives of Windsor,* Doctor Caius: "Mock-vater! $\overline{79}\ \overline{74}\ \overline{43}$ is dat?"

X. *King Henry the Fifth,* Pistol: "A lad of life, an imp of fame; of parents good, of $\overline{122}\ \overline{6}\ \overline{21}\ \overline{115}$ most valiant."

Y. *King Lear,* King Lear: "That fellow handles his $\overline{109}\ \overline{126}\ \overline{37}$ like a crow-keeper: draw me a clothier's yard."

Z. *Romeo and Juliet,* Juliet: "Now is the sun upon the highmost $\overline{34}\ \overline{9}\ \overline{23}\ \overline{67}$ of this day's journey."

1 C	2 B	3 M	4 D	5 J		6 X	7 Q		8 I	9 Z	10 D	11 A		12 E	13 P	14 G	
15 H	16 G	17 L	18 M	19 Q	20 B	21 X		22 B	23 Z	24 D	25 T	26 H	27 P	28 V	29 L		30 K
31 N	32 U		33 N	34 Z	35 Q	36 F		37 Y	38 B	39 E	40 K		41 R	42 T	43 W		44 G
45 R		46 U	47 D	48 N	49 J	50 E	51 U	52 C	53 H	54 L	55 Q	56 F	57 A		58 K	59 D	60 H
61 V		62 F	63 S	64 J	65 O	66 H		67 Z	68 I	69 R	70 Q	71 B		72 I	73 R	74 W	75 D
76 A		77 M	78 G	79 W	80 J		81 M	82 P	83 O	84 S	85 B	86 V	87 T'	88 A	89 D		90 P
91 L	92 M	93 B	94 T	95 A	96 N	97 H		98 E	99 R	100 K	101 C		102 S	103 I	104 N		105 S
106 O	107 G	108 I		109 W	110 F	111 O	112 L		113 E	114 N	115 X	116 L	117 K	118 G	119 D	120 C	121 K
	122 X	123 J	124 U	125 A		126 Y	127 F	128 D	129 G	130 J	131 J		132 A	133 D	134 H	135 L	136 V

Alcibiades.
From Guillaume Rouille, *Promptuarii iconum* (1553).

ANSWERS

Game 1
The play's the thing

1. Bernardo, *Hamlet*
2. Shipmaster, *The Tempest*
3. Poet, *Timon of Athens*
4. Duke of Buckingham, *King Henry the Eighth*
5. First Gentleman, *Cymbeline*
6. Earl of Kent, *King Lear*
7. Philo, *Antony and Cleopatra*
8. Earl of Warwick, *King Henry the Sixth, Part Three*
9. Duke, *Measure for Measure*
10. Rumour, *King Henry the Fourth, Part Two*
11. Valentine, *The Two Gentlemen of Verona*
12. Saturninus, *Titus Andronicus*
13. Shallow, *The Merry Wives of Windsor*
14. First Citizen, *Coriolanus*
15. Duke of Illyria, *Twelfth Night*
16. Leonato, *Much Ado About Nothing*
17. Aegeon, *The Comedy of Errors*
18. King, *Love's Labour's Lost*
19. Flavius, *Julius Caesar*
20. First Witch, *Macbeth*
21. Chorus, *Troilus and Cressida*

Game 2
Methodical madness

1. The Winter's Tale
2. Romeo and Juliet
3. The Taming of the Shrew
4. King Lear
5. Julius Caesar
6. Measure for Measure
7. The Comedy of Errors
8. Othello
9. As You Like It
10. Much Ado About Nothing
11. Timon of Athens
12. The Tempest

Game 3
Disordered wit

1. " 'Tis but thy name that is my enemy;—thou art thyself though, not a Montague." (Juliet, *Romeo and Juliet,* Act 2, Scene 1)
2. "The quality of mercy is not strained,—it droppeth as the gentle rain from heaven upon the place beneath." (Portia, *The Merchant of Venice,* Act 4, Scene 1)
3. "Now is the winter of our discontent made glorious summer by this sun of York." (Duke of Gloucester, *King Richard the Third,* Act 1, Scene 1)
4. "What fates impose, that men must needs abide." (King Edward, *King Henry the Sixth, Part Three,* Act 4, Scene 3)
5. "She's beautiful and therefore to be woo'd; she is a woman, therefore to be won." (Earl of Suffolk, *King Henry the Sixth, Part One,* Act 5, Scene 3)
6. "My lips, two blushing pilgrims, ready stand to smooth that rough touch with a tender kiss." (Romeo) "Good pilgrim, you do wrong your hand too much." (Juliet, *Romeo and Juliet,* Act 1, Scene 5)
7. "This England never did, nor never shall, lie at the proud foot of a conqueror." (Bastard, *King John,* Act 5, Scene 7)

8. "Rebellion lay in his way, and he found it." (Sir John Falstaff, *King Henry the Fourth, Part One,* Act 5, Scene 1)

9. "The fault, dear Brutus, is not in our stars." (Cassius, *Julius Caesar,* Act 1, Scene 2)

10. "Men are April when they woo, December when they wed." (Rosalind, *As You Like It,* Act 4, Scene 1)

11. "But men are men; the best sometimes forget." (Iago, *Othello,* Act 2, Scene 3)

12. "Few love to hear the sins they love to act." (Pericles, *Pericles,* Act 1, Scene 1)

Game 4
A sea of choices

1. "Screw your courage to the sticking place." (Lady Macbeth, *Macbeth,* Act 1, Scene 7)

2. "Parting is such sweet sorrow, that I shall say good night till it be morrow." (Juliet, *Romeo and Juliet,* Act 2, Scene 1)

3. "He thinks too much: Such men are dangerous." (Julius Caesar, *Julius Caesar,* Act 1, Scene 2)

4. "Sleep, that knits up the ravell'd sleave of care." (Macbeth, *Macbeth,* Act 2, Scene 2)

5. "My salad days; when I was green in judgement." (Cleopatra, *Antony and Cleopatra,* Act 1, Scene 5)

6. "But I will wear my heart upon my sleeve for daws to peck at." (Iago, *Othello,* Act 1, Scene 1)

7. "One that loved not wisely but too well." (Othello, *Othello,* Act 5, Scene 2)

8. "Yet do I fear thy nature; it is too full of the milk of human kindness." (Lady Macbeth, *Macbeth,* Act 1, Scene 5)

9. "How sharper than a serpent's tooth it is to have a thankless child." (King Lear, *King Lear,* Act 1, Scene 4)

10. "Choked with ambition of the meaner sort." (Mortimer,

King Henry the Sixth, Part One, Act 2, Scene 5)

11. "Speak again, bright angel!" (Romeo, *Romeo and Juliet,* Act 2, Scene 2)

12. "Cowards die many times before their deaths; the valiant never taste of death but once." (Julius Caesar, *Julius Caesar,* Act 2, Scene 2)

Game 5

Confuse thy name

1. Ophelia
2. Petruchio
3. Falstaff
4. Desdemona
5. Guildenstern
6. Polonius
7. Polixenes
8. Violenta
9. Touchstone
10. Lady Macbeth
11. Earl of Gloucester
12. Edgar
13. Portia
14. Perdita
15. Valentine
16. Duke of Cornwall
17. Hotspur
18. Benvolio
19. Bottom
20. Escalus
21. Proteus
22. Panthino
23. Biron
24. Costard
25. Rosaline
26. Balthasar
27. Starveling
28. Hortensio
29. Don Pedro
30. Dogberry
31. Mistress Page
32. Sebastian
33. Goneril
34. Cleopatra
35. Armado

Game 6
Deceitful words

1. c: struts. Fabian, *Twelfth Night,* Act 2, Scene 5
2. d: lightly armed footsoldiers. King Richard, *King Richard the Second,* Act 2, Scene 1
3. b: a clock. Iago, *Othello,* Act 2, Scene 3
4. b: a grimace. Ariel, *The Tempest,* Act 4, Scene 1
5. a: shoved. Iago, *Othello,* Act 1, Scene 2
6. c: a display. Gratiano, *The Merchant of Venice,* Act 2, Scene 2
7. a: fist. Pistol, *King Henry the Fourth, Part Two,* Act 2, Scene 4
8. d: know. Antony, *Antony and Cleopatra,* Act 1, Scene 1
9. b: lazy fellow. Prince Henry, *King Henry the Fourth, Part One,* Act 2, Scene 4
10. c: drunk. Bardolph, *The Merry Wives of Windsor,* Act 1, Scene 1
11. a: defame. Armado, *Love's Labour's Lost,* Act 5, Scene 2
12. b: a harmless weapon. Michael Williams, *King Henry the Fifth,* Act 4, Scene 1
13. d: use trickery. Macbeth, *Macbeth,* Act 5, Scene 8
14. c: protection. Benedick and Claudio, *Much Ado About Nothing,* Act 1, Scene 1
15. c: lewd person. Bertram, *All's Well That Ends Well,* Act 5, Scene 3

Game 7
Star-crossed lovers

1. D (Petruchio and Katharina) Act 2, Scene 1
2. E (Mark Antony and Cleopatra) Act 1, Scene 1
3. F (Romeo and Juliet) Act 2, Scene 1
4. B (Bassanio and Portia) Act 3, Scene 2

5. G (Benedick and Beatrice) Act 1, Scene 1

6. C (Troilus and Cressida) Act 4, Scene 4

7. A (Florizel and Perdita) Act 4, Scene 3

Game 8

What employment have we here?

ARCHER: 2. Antiochus, *Pericles* (Act 1, Scene 1). 1. Sir Walter Scott. 3. Charles Baudelaire.

COOK: 1. Pompey, *Antony and Cleopatra* (Act 2, Scene 1). 2. Saki. 3. Robert Burton.

MERCHANT: 2. Baptista, *The Taming of the Shrew* (Act 2, Scene 1). 1. Thomas Jefferson. 3. Emily Dickinson.

SOLDIER: 3. Cymbeline, *Cymbeline* (Act 5, Scene 5). 1. General George Patton. 2. Voltaire.

ARCHITECT: 3. Marcus Andronicus, *Titus Andronicus* (Act 5, Scene 3). 1. Sallust. 2. Johann von Goethe.

TEACHER: 2. Armado, *Love's Labour's Lost* (Act 5, Scene 2). 1. Amos Alcott. 3. Oliver Goldsmith.

DOCTOR: 1. Cymbeline, *Cymbeline* (Act 5, Scene 5). 2. Benjamin Franklin. 3. Lord Byron.

BUTCHER: 3. Imogen, *Cymbeline* (Act 3, Scene 4). 1. John Aubrey (written about Shakespeare). 2. Carl Sandburg.

LAWYER: 2. Dick the Butcher, *King Henry the Sixth, Part Two* (Act 4, Scene 2). 1. Daniel Webster. 3. Edmund Burke.

CLERK: 1. Cardinal Wolsey, *King Henry the Eighth* (Act 2, Scene 2). 2. Alexander Pope. 3. Ihara Saikaku.

ACTOR: 2. Bottom, *A Midsummer Night's Dream* (Act 4, Scene 2). 1. Sir Winston Churchill. 3. Carl Jung.

WRITER: 3. Domitius Enobarbus, *Antony and Cleopatra* (Act 3, Scene 2). 1. Robert Frost. 2. Samuel Johnson.

Game 9
Mine enemies

1. F (Macbeth and Macduff) Act 5, Scene 8
2. G (Hamlet and Laertes) Act 5, Scene 2
3. E (Tybalt and Mercutio) Act 3, Scene 1
4. A (Duke of Cornwall and Earl of Gloucester) Act 3, Scene 7
5. B (Thurio and Valentine) Act 2, Scene 4
6. C (Hotspur and Prince Henry) Act 5, Scene 4
7. D (Edgar and Edmund) Act 5, Scene 3

Game 10
Merely players

1. b
2. d
3. a

4. c
5. b

Game 11
Cakes and ale

APPETIZER
1. Shakespeare: Pistol, *The Merry Wives of Windsor*, Act 2, Scene 2
2. John Heywood
3. Shakespeare: Sir John Falstaff, *King Henry the Fourth, Part One*, Act 2, Scene 4
4. Shakespeare: Clown, *All's Well That Ends Well*, Act 4, Scene 5
5. William Butler Yeats

ENTREE
1. W. S. Gilbert
2. Shakespeare: Clown, *All's Well That Ends Well,* Act 5, Scene 2
3. William Makepeace Thackeray
4. Richard Leveridge
5. Shakespeare: Christopher Sly, *The Taming of the Shrew,* Introduction, Scene 2
6. Anatole France
7. Shakespeare: Grumio and Katharina, *The Taming of the Shrew,* Act 4, Scene 3
8. Shakespeare: Cressida, *Troilus and Cressida,* Act 1, Scene 2
9. Lady Mary Wortley Montagu
10. King Henry IV of France
11. Shakespeare: Hamlet, *Hamlet,* Act 2, Scene 2
12. Shakespeare: Dromio of Ephesus, *The Comedy of Errors,* Act 1, Scene 2

SIDE DISH
1. Shakespeare: Second carrier, *King Henry the Fourth, Part One,* Act 2, Scene 1
2. Charles Dickens
3. Shakespeare: Boyet, *Love's Labour's Lost,* Act 2, Scene 1
4. Shakespeare: Poins, *King Henry the Fourth, Part One,* Act 1, Scene 2
5. W. S. Gilbert
6. Shakespeare: Second Carrier, *King Henry the Fourth, Part One,* Act 2, Scene 1

BREAD AND CHEESE
1. A. A. Milne
2. Shakespeare: King Henry, *King Henry the Fifth,* Act 4, Scene 1
3. Shakespeare: First Citizen, *Coriolanus,* Act 1, Scene 1

4. Juvenal
5. Henry James
6. Shakespeare: Lucio, *Measure for Measure,* Act 3, Scene 2
7. Shakespeare: Sir John Falstaff, *The Merry Wives of Windsor,* Act 5, Scene 5
8. Eugene Field
9. Anthelme Brillat-Savarin
10. Shakespeare: Sir Hugh Evans, *The Merry Wives of Windsor,* Act 1, Scene 2

BEER AND WINE
1. Shakespeare: Third Neighbour, *King Henry the Sixth, Part Two,* Act 2, Scene 3
2. Samuel Johnson
3. Thomas Hughes
4. Shakespeare: Prince Henry, *King Henry the Fourth, Part Two,* Act 1, Scene 1
5. A. E. Housman
6. Shakespeare: Autolycus, *The Winter's Tale,* Act 4, Scene 3
7. Shakespeare: Hostess Quickly, *King Henry the Fourth, Part Two,* Act 2, Scene 4
8. Ernest Dowson
9. Emily Dickinson
10. Shakespeare: Silence, *King Henry the Fourth, Part Two,* Act 5, Scene 3

DESSERT
1. John Greenleaf Whittier
2. Shakespeare: Petruchio, *The Taming of the Shrew,* Act 4, Scene 3
3. Shakespeare: Doll Tear-Sheet, *King Henry the Fourth, Part Two,* Act 2, Scene 4
4. Charles Dickens
5. H. W. and F. G. Fowler

6. Edward Taylor

7. Shakespeare: Pandarus, *Troilus and Cressida,* Act 1, Scene 1

8. Shakespeare: Touchstone, *As You Like It,* Act 3, Scene 3

BEVERAGE

1. Shakespeare: Biron and Princess, *Love's Labour's Lost,* Act 5, Scene 2

2. W. S. Gilbert

3. Shakespeare: Hotspur, *King Henry the Fourth, Part One,* Act 2, Scene 3

4. Punch

5. G. K. Chesterton

6. Wallace Stevens

7. T. S. Eliot

Game 12
To steal their brains

1. b

2. d

3. a

4. c

5. c

Game 13
Fool's play

1. J (Caphis and Apemantus) Act 2, Scene 2

2. D (Lear and the Fool) Act 1, Scene 4

3. E (Parolles and the Clown) Act 2, Scene 4

4. I (Sir Andrew Aguecheek and the Clown) Act 2, Scene 3

5. F (Proteus and Julia) Act 5, Scene 2

6. K (Earl of Kent and the Fool) Act 1, Scene 4

7. L (Varro's Servant and the Fool) Act 2, Scene 2

8. B (Biron and Rosaline) Act 2, Scene 1
9. H (Touchstone and Rosalind) Act 2, Scene 4
10. G (Achilles and Thersites) Act 2, Scene 1
11. A (Launcelot and Lorenzo) Act 3, Scene 5
12. C (Earl of Kent and the Fool) Act 2, Scene 4

Game 14
Strange bedfellows

1. a, c, g, h, i, j
2. c
3. a, b, c, e, g, h
4. a

5. d
6. b, e, g, h
7. c, d, h, j
8. b

Game 15
A caldron boiling

1. S
2. D
3. J
4. M
5. F
6. N
7. E
8. G
9. O
10. A

11. H
12. K
13. P
14. L
15. B
16. I
17. Q
18. R
19. C

Game 16
Garden sport

1. Shakespeare: Iago, *Othello,* Act 1, Scene 3
2. Johann von Goethe
3. Edmund Spenser
4. Robert Herrick
5. Shakespeare: Perdita, *The Winter's Tale,* Act 4, Scene 3
6. William Morris
7. Shakespeare: Ophelia, *Hamlet,* Act 4, Scene 5
8. Shakespeare: Earl of Salisbury, *King John,* Act 4, Scene 2
9. Gertrude Stein
10. Shakespeare: Gadshill, *King Henry the Fourth, Part One,* Act 2, Scene 1
11. Archibald MacLeish
12. Shakespeare: Adriana, *The Comedy of Errors,* Act 2, Scene 2
13. Shakespeare: Puck, *A Midsummer Night's Dream,* Act 2, Scene 1
14. Shakespeare: Sir John Falstaff, *King Henry the Fourth, Part One,* Act 2, Scene 4
15. James Whitcomb Riley
16. Shakespeare: Duke of Gloucester, *King Richard the Third,* Act 3, Scene 4
17. Shakespeare: Biondello, *The Taming of the Shrew,* Act 4, Scene 4
18. William Bliss Carman
19. Shakespeare: Gardener, *King Richard the Second,* Act 3, Scene 4
20. Samuel Eliot Morison
21. Shakespeare: First Servant, *King Richard the Second,* Act 3, Scene 4
22. Mao Tse-tung
23. Herman Melville

24. Shakespeare: Isabella, *Measure for Measure,* Act 2, Scene 2

25. Rudyard Kipling

Game 17
All's well that ends well

1. c: Act 3, Scene 3
2. d: Act 5, Scene 4
3. b: Act 5, Scene 1
4. e: Act 1, Scene 2
5. d: Act 2, Scene 2
6. c: Act 4, Scene 2
7. b: Act 2, Scene 3
8. e: Act 3, Scene 2
9. a: Act 1, Scene 1
10. d: Act 4, Scene 1

Game 18
A rose by any other name

1. c: Act 5, Scene 1
2. b: Act 2, Scene 3
3. d: Act 3, Scene 1
4. b: Act 2, Scene 2
5. a: Act 2, Scene 1
6. c: Act 2, Scene 2
7. b: Act 5, Scene 3
8. d: Act 4, Scene 1
9. a: Act 1, Scene 7
10. c: Act 2, Scene 1
11. c: Act 3, Scene 3
12. d

Game 19
A false creation

1. "There is a tide in the affairs of men which, taken at the <u>flood</u>, leads on to <u>fortune</u>." (Marcus Brutus, *Julius Caesar,* Act 4, Scene 3)

2. "Brevity is the soul of wit." (Polonius, *Hamlet,* Act 2, Scene 2)

3. "The empty <u>vessel</u> makes the greatest sound." (Boy, *King*

Henry the Fifth, Act 4, Scene 4)

4. "He that <u>dies</u> pays all debts."(Stephano, *The Tempest,* Act 3, Scene 2)

5. "Uneasy lies the head that wears a <u>crown</u>." (King Henry, *King Henry the Fourth, Part Two,* Act 3, Scene 1)

6. "The evil that men do lives after them; the <u>good</u> is oft interred with their bones."(Marcus Antonius, *Julius Caesar,* Act 3, Scene 2)

7. "Fight till the last <u>gasp</u>." (Joan La Pucelle, *King Henry the Sixth, Part One,* Act 1, Scene 2)

8. "There is no <u>vice</u> so simple, but assumes some mark of <u>virtue</u> on his outward parts." (Bassanio, *The Merchant of Venice,* Act 3, Scene 2)

9. "A good mouth-filling <u>oath</u>." (Hotspur, *King Henry the Fourth, Part One,* Act 3, Scene 1)

10. "He shows me where the bachelors sit, and there live we as <u>merry</u> as the day is long." (Beatrice, *Much Ado About Nothing,* Act 2, Scene 1)

11. "This is very midsummer <u>madness</u>."(Olivia, *Twelfth Night,* Act 3, Scene 4)

12. "O, that men's <u>ears</u> should be to counsel deaf, but not to flattery!(Apemantus, *Timon of Athens,* Act 1, Scene 2)

Game 20
The course of true love

1. Ovid
2. Shakespeare: Armado, *Love's Labour's Lost,* Act 1, Scene 2
3. Shakespeare: Mistress Page, *The Merry Wives of Windsor,* Act 2, Scene 1
4. Henry Fielding
5. Shakespeare: Rosalind, *As You Like It,* Act 3, Scene 5
6. Rudyard Kipling

7. William Penn
8. Lord Byron
9. Shakespeare: Sonnet 116
10. Shakespeare: Sonnet 119
11. Shakespeare: Romeo, *Romeo and Juliet,* Act 1, Scene 1
12. Robert Frost
13. Shakespeare: Duke of Illyria, *Twelfth Night,* Act 2, Scene 4
14. Shakespeare: Silvius, *As You Like It,* Act 2, Scene 4
15. Alexander Pope
16. Shakespeare: Goneril, *King Lear,* Act 1, Scene 1
17. W. H. Auden
18. Dorothy Parker
19. Shakespeare: Hotspur, *King Henry the Fourth, Part One,* Act 2, Scene 3
20. Emily Dickinson

Game 21
What's in a name?

1. Robin	2. Paris	3. Basset	4. Audrey
Poins	Cinna	Dromio	Olivia
Timon	Henry	Grumio	Blount
Helen	Percy	Pistol	Gurney
Lucio	Belch	Rumour	Thaisa
		Jaques	Angelo

Game 22

Quirky pens

1. a. "That every nice offence should bear his comment."
   b. "For every inch of woman in the world."
   c. "He is a better scholar than I thought he was."
   d. "What care these roarers for the name of king?"
   Lear, *King Lear,* Act 4, Scene 6

2. a. "A most unnoble swerving."
   b. "A plague upon this howling."
   c. "This quarry cries on havoc."
   d. "Two households, both alike in dignity."
   e. "You have receiv'd your gifts."
   f. "If these be good people in a commonweal that do nothing but use their abuses in common houses."
   Mercutio, *Romeo and Juliet,* Act 3, Scene 1

3. a. "What a life dost thou lead!"
   b. "A horse cannot fetch, but only carry."
   c. " 'Tis not the trial of a woman's war."
   d. "For a hawk, a horse, or a husband."
   e. "By my troth, we that have good wits have much to answer for."
   f. "This will prove a brave kingdom to me."
   g. "Hang her up for ever!"
   h. "I can keep honest counsel, ride, run, mar a curious tale in telling it."
   i. "I pray you, stay not, but in haste to horse."
   King Richard, *King Richard the Third,* Act 5, Scene 4

4. a. "That very envy and the tongue of loss."
   b. "And thereby for sealing the injury of tongues in courts and kingdoms."
   c. "What passion hangs these weights upon my tongue?"
   d. "It may be his enemy is a gentleman of great sort."
   e. "Your tale, sir, would cure deafness."
   Jaques, *As You Like It,* Act 2, Scene 7

Game 23

Pun thee into shivers

1. Mistress Quickly, *The Merry Wives of Windsor*
2. Albany, *King Lear*
3. Fabian, *Twelfth Night*
4. Ajax, *Troilus and Cressida*
5. Elbow, *Measure for Measure*
6. Lincoln, *King Henry the Eighth*
7. Crab the dog, *The Two Gentlemen of Verona*
8. Bourbon, *King Henry the Fifth*
9. Fang, *King Henry the Sixth, Part Two*
10. Shallow, *The Merry Wives of Windsor*
11. Speed, *The Two Gentlemen of Verona*
12. Paris, *Troilus and Cressida*
13. Dull, *Love's Labour's Lost*
14. Pistol, *The Merry Wives of Windsor*
15. Rugby, *The Merry Wives of Windsor*

Game 24

A grievous fault

1. Sonnet No. 53: The structural flaw in this sonnet is that within each quatrain the four lines are written in reverse order. The two lines of the couplet are also reversed. The sonnet should read:

> What is your substance, whereof are you made,
> That millions of strange shadows on you tend?
> Since every one hath, every one, one shade,
> And you, but one, can every shadow lend.
> Describe Adonis, and the counterfeit
> Is poorly imitated after you;

On Helen's cheek all art of beauty set,
And you in Grecian tires are painted new:
Speak of the spring, and foison of the year;
The one doth shadow of your beauty show,
The other as your bounty doth appear;
And you in every blessed shape we know.
>In all external grace you have some part,
>But you like none, none you, for constant heart.

2. Sonnet No. 14: The flaw here is that lines 1–12 are written in reverse order. The couplet is correct as written. The sonnet should read:
Not from the stars do I my judgment pluck;
And yet methinks I have astronomy,
But not to tell of good or evil luck,
Of plagues, of dearths, or seasons' quality;
Nor can I fortune to brief minutes tell,
Pointing to each his thunder, rain, and wind,
Or say with princes if it shall go well,
By oft predict that I in heaven find:
But from thine eyes my knowledge I derive,
And, constant stars, in them I read such art,
As truth and beauty shall together thrive,
If from thyself to store thou wouldst convert;
>Or else of thee this I prognosticate:
>Thy end is truth's and beauty's doom and date.

3. Sonnet No. 122: Each line, except for the rhyming word, is switched with the one below it. The sonnet should read:
Thy gift, thy tables, are within my brain
Full character'd with lasting memory,
Which shall above that idle rank remain,
Beyond all date, even to eternity:
Or, at the least, so long as brain and heart
Have faculty by nature to subsist;
Till each to raz'd oblivion yield his part
Of thee, thy record never can be miss'd.

That poor retention could not so much hold,
Nor need I tallies thy dear love to score;
Therefore to give them from me was I bold,
To trust those tables that receive thee more:
    To keep an adjunct to remember thee
    Were to import forgetfulness in me.

Game 25
Impassioned confusion

1. Lady Macbeth, *Macbeth,* Act 5, Scene 1
    "Out, damned spot! I say!—One two; why, then 'tis time to do't:—Hell is murky!—Fie, my lord, fie! a soldier, and afeard? What need we fear who knows it, when none can call our power to account?—Yet who would have thought the old man to have had so much blood in him?"

2. Marcus Antonius, *Julius Caesar,* Act 3, Scene 1
"O, pardon me, thou bleeding piece of earth,
That I am meek and gentle with these butchers!
Thou art the ruins of the noblest man
That ever lived in the tide of times.
Woe to the hand that shed this costly blood!"

3. John of Gaunt, *King Richard the Second,* Act 2, Scene 1
"This royal throne of kings, this scepter'd isle,
This earth of majesty, this seat of Mars,
This other Eden, demi-Paradise;
This fortress built by Nature for herself
Against infection and the hand of war;
This happy breed of men, this little world;
This precious stone set in the silver sea,
Which serves it in the office of a wall,
Or as a moat defensive to a house,
Against the envy of less happier lands;
This blessed plot, this earth, this realm, this England."

Game 26
All the world's a stage

1. K (Romeo–Juliet, *Romeo and Juliet*, Act 2, Scene 2)
2. A (John of Gaunt, *King Richard the Second*, Act 2, Scene 1)
3. L (Shylock, *The Merchant of Venice*, Act 3, Scene 1)
4. F (Hamlet, *Hamlet*, Act 2, Scene 2)
5. G (Helena, *All's Well That Ends Well*, Act 4, Scene 4)
6. D (Lady Macbeth–Macbeth, *Macbeth*, Act 2, Scene 2)
7. H (Doctor–Lady Macbeth, *Macbeth*, Act 5, Scene 1)
8. C (Duke Senior–Jaques, *As You Like It*, Act 2, Scene 7)
9. I (Julius Caesar–Soothsayer, *Julius Caesar*, Act 1, Scene 2)
10. B (Cassius, *Julius Caesar*, Act 1, Scene 2)
11. J (Citizens–Marcus Antonius, *Julius Caesar*, Act 3, Scene 2)
12. E (Sir William Catesby–King Richard, *King Richard the Third*, Act 5, Scene 4)

Game 27
Wild talk

FIRST SCENE: *Cymbeline*, Act 5, Scene 5:

1. Imogen
2. Posthumus Leonatus
3. Pisanio
4. Cymbeline
5. Posthumus Leonatus
6. Pisanio
7. Cymbeline
8. Pisanio
9. Imogen

SECOND SCENE: *The Tempest*, Act 2, Scene 1:

1. Alonso
2. Sebastian
3. Antonio
4. Sebastian
5. Gonzalo
6. Sebastian

7. Gonzalo   **10.** Sebastian

8. Sebastian   **11.** Gonzalo

9. Gonzalo   **12.** Antonio

THIRD SCENE, the random scene chosen by the dice:

1. Hermione, *The Winter's Tale*
2. Sir Hugh Evans, *The Merry Wives of Windsor*
3. Antipholus of Ephesus, *The Comedy of Errors*
4. Octavius Caesar, *Antony and Cleopatra*
5. Henry Bolingbroke, *King Richard the Second*
6. Sebastian, *Twelfth Night*
7. Regan, *King Lear*
8. Angelo, *Measure for Measure*
9. Lucentio, *The Taming of the Shrew*
10. Angelo, *The Comedy of Errors*
11. Imogen, *Cymbeline*
12. Cerimon, *Pericles*
13. Armado, *Love's Labour's Lost*
14. Charles, *King Henry the Sixth, Part One*
15. Tyrian Sailor, *Pericles*

Game 28
The seeming truth

1. Sonnet No. 92
2. The random sonnet: First quatrain: from Sonnet No. 28
   Second quatrain: from Sonnet No. 104

   Third quatrain: from Sonnet No. 25
   The couplet: from Sonnet No. 87

3. Sonnet No. 37

Game 29
Upon thy stars

1. b: Act 4, Scene 3   **4.** a: Act 1, Scene 2

2. d: Act 3, Scene 2   **5.** c: Act 5, Scene 4

3. b: Act 1, Scene 3

Game 30
Finish the jest

1. Octavius Caesar, *Julius Caesar*
2. Earl of Warwick, *King Henry the Sixth, Part Two*
3. King Edward, *King Henry the Sixth, Part Three*
4. King Henry, *King Henry the Fourth, Part One*
5. Fortinbras, *Hamlet*
6. Cymbeline, *Cymbeline*
7. Armado, *Love's Labour's Lost*
8. Dromio of Ephesus, *The Comedy of Errors*
9. Puck, *A Midsummer Night's Dream*
10. Henry Bolingbroke, *King Richard the Second*
11. Duke Vincentio, *Measure for Measure*
12. Prospero, *The Tempest*
13. Edgar, *King Lear*
14. Clown, *Twelfth Night*
15. Gower, *Pericles*

Double Crostic 1
Double, double

A. beefwitted

B. mow

C. Holofernes

D. phrases

E. rude

F. haughty

G. regard

H. fat

I. hallowmass

J. wine

K. bed

L. raisins

M. books

N. rawboned

O. Hermia

P. weed

Q. whether

R. thrifty

S. voluntary

T. terrestrial

U. tender

V. heath

W. thitherward

X. season

Y. heart

Z. thread

Z1. seeming

Z2. troth

Z3. nonce

Z4. shiver

Z5. nonpareil

Z6. shelter

QUOTE: Benedick, *Much Ado About Nothing*:
"She speaks poniards and every word stabs. If her breath were as terrible as her terminations, there were no living near her. She would infect to the north star. I would not marry her though she were endowed with all that Adam had left him before he transgrest."

Double Crostic 2
Toil and trouble

A. beldame   N. untrue

B. tidings   O. scan

C. star   P. hoop

D. likelihood   Q. shake

E. stale   R. venom

F. taste   S. twas

G. bereave   T. proud

H. history   U. done

I. loose   V. shun

J. surrey   W. vat

K. Wolsey   X. fist

L. shackle   Y. bow

M. vouch   Z. hill

QUOTE: Biron, from *Love's Labour's Lost*:
"Study is like the heaven's glorious sun, that will not be deep-searched with saucy looks. Small have continual plodders ever won save base authority from others' books."

Answers to
Bonus Games

Game **1**: Quote. Hamlet, *Hamlet,* Act 2, Scene 2.

Game **2**: Paraphrase. "Though this be madness, yet there is method in't." Polonius, *Hamlet,* Act 2, Scene 2.

Game **3**: Paraphrase. "There is such disorder in my wit." Constance, *King John,* Act 3, Scene 4.

Game **4**: Paraphrase. "A sea of troubles." Hamlet, *Hamlet,* Act 3, Scene 1.

Game **5**: Paraphrase. "Refuse thy name." Juliet, *Romeo and Juliet,* Act 2, Scene 2.

Game **6**: Paraphrase. "The folded meaning of your word's deceit." Syracusa, *The Comedy of Errors,* Act 3, Scene 2.

Graphic Game **1**: Quote. Hamlet, *Hamlet,* Act 3, Scene 1.

Game **7**: Quote. Chorus, *Romeo and Juliet,* Prologue.

Game **8**: Quote. Malvolio, *Twelfth Night,* Act 2, Scene 5.

Game **9**: Quote. Prospero, *The Tempest,* Act 3, Scene 3.

Game **10**: Quote. Jaques, *As You Like It,* Act 2, Scene 2.

Game **11**: Quote. Sir Toby Belch, *Twelfth Night,* Act 2, Scene 3.

Game **12**: Paraphrase. "To steal away their brains." Cassio, *Othello,* Act 2, Scene 3.

Graphic Game **2**: Quote. Achilles, *Troilus and Cressida,* Act 5, Scene 6.

Game **13**: Paraphrase. "Let me play the fool." Gratiano, *The Merchant of Venice,* Act 1, Scene 1.

Game **14**: Quote. Trinculo, *The Tempest,* Act 2, Scene 2.

Game **15**: Quote. Stage direction, *Macbeth,* Act 4, Scene 1.

Game **16**: Paraphrase. "What sport shall we devise in this garden?" Queen, *King Richard the Second,* Act 3, Scene 4.

Game **17:** Quote. Helen, *All's Well That Ends Well*, Act 4, Scene 4.

Game **18:** Quote. Juliet, *Romeo and Juliet*, Act 2, Scene 2.

Graphic Game **3:** Quote. Juliet, *Romeo and Juliet*, Act 2, Scene 2.

Game **19:** Quote. Macbeth, *Macbeth*, Act 2, Scene 1.

Game **20:** Quote. Lysander, *A Midsummer Night's Dream*, Act 1, Scene 1.

Game **21:** Quote. Juliet, *Romeo and Juliet*, Act 2, Scene 2.

Game **22:** Paraphrase. "The quirks of blazoning pens." Cassio, *Othello*, Act 2, Scene 1.

Game **23:** Quote. Thersites, *Troilus and Cressida*, Act 2, Scene 1.

Graphic Game **4:** Duke of Burgundy, *King Henry the Sixth, Part One*, Act 2, Scene 2.

Game **24:** Quote. Marc Antony, *Julius Caesar*, Act 3, Scene 2.

Game **25:** Paraphrase. "I never heard a passion so confused." Solanio, *The Merchant of Venice*, Act 2, Scene 8.

Game **26:** Quote. Jaques, *As You Like It*, Act 2, Scene 7.

Game **27:** Paraphrase. "If I chance to talk a little wild, forgive me." Lord Sands, *King Henry the Eighth*, Act 1, Scene 4.

Game **28:** Quote. Bassanio, *Merchant of Venice*, Act 3, Scene 1.

Game **29:** Quote. Constance, *King John*, Act 3, Scene 1.

Game **30:** Quote. Katherine, *Love's Labour's Lost*, Act 2, Scene 1.

Graphic Game **5:** Quote. Witches, *Macbeth*, Act 4, Scene 1.

Graphic Game **6:** Quote. Witches, *Macbeth*, Act 4, Scene 1.